Recollections: A Baby Boomer's Memories of the Fabulous Fifties

Jim Chambers

ISBN: 978-0-557-09100-3

Front cover photographs are from Wikimedia Commons.

CONTENTS

ACKNOWLEDGMENTS

FOREWORD

Chapter 1 .... War – The Aftermath

Chapter 2 .... The Family

Chapter 3 .... Kids Only

Chapter 4 .... School

Chapter 5 .... Arts and Entertainment

Chapter 6 .... Politics and Culture

Chapter 7 .... Shopping

Chapter 8 .... Gadgets and Gizmos

Chapter 9 .... Food, Glorious Food

Chapter 10 .... Transportation and Travel

Chapter 11 .... On the Road to Equality

Chapter 12 .... War (Hot and Cold)

End Notes

About the Author

ACKNOWLEDGEMENTS

This book is dedicated to the two women in my life who have had profound influences on me. First, my mother Verna Chambers, who worked relentlessly to impart a love of reading and learning in me; and second, my wife Deborah, who keeps me straight and is the very definition of a soulmate. I hate to imagine what my life would have been like without them.

I'd better not fail to mention my three sisters, Janis, Jean, and Susan, or they'll yell at me. I was the firstborn and the only son, so they all look up to me and worship the ground I walk on. Actually, that may be stretching it just a wee bit, but this is my book, and they're free to write their own dissenting opinions! In any case, we all get along wonderfully today.

FOREWORD

What if the hokey pokey really is what it's all about?

One of my favorite books is *The Life and Times of the Thunderbolt Kid*, a humorous memoir by Bill Bryson of his childhood years growing up in the 1950s and early 1960s. Bill did a marvelous job of describing how it was to be a kid in the United States during that period. I was born in 1946, so the 1950s were my coming of age decade too. There were some major differences in our lives, however. Bill grew up in the Midwest (Des Moines, Iowa), and I was born and raised in the South (Atlanta, Georgia), so we had somewhat different perspectives on our times. Also, Bill had a brother and a sister, whereas I had three sisters, and believe me, that was a colossal difference.

Many of the incidents in *The Life and Times of the Thunderbolt Kid* were reminiscent of my own youth, and they brought back a flood of recollections. Reading the book brought back a lot of childhood memories that I had forgotten, memories of what it was like to grow up in that exciting decade. World War II had ended a few months before I was born, and I was one of the first Baby Boomers, born nine months after my father returned from serving with the US Army Air Corps in England.

The end of World War II was a time for celebration, especially when our military men returned to the US and were discharged to rejoin civilian life. Returning GIs, airmen, marines, and sailors were treated as heroes, but after a while the ticker tape parades were over and everyone got back to work. Things weren't the same as before the war. Boys left for the war and returned as men who had been in hell. Some never returned, being buried in cemeteries in far-flung places. Women had gone to work in factories and learned to be far more independent-minded than their mothers. And the war ended the Great

Depression, which had shaped the lives of everyone living in that era.

The 1950s should have been a peaceful decade, but suddenly our wartime enemies became our allies and our allies became our enemies, and we were fighting again, this time in South Korea in 1951. It was the decade when the Cold War with the Communists dominated geopolitics, and nuclear Armageddon became a very real threat to our existence. Old colonial empires were breaking up, and the world was being dramatically reshaped.

In the 1950s, scientists, researchers, and engineers gave us a huge variety of new discoveries and creations, from the hydrogen bomb to the transistor radio, and television created a nation of couch potatoes. The double helix structure of DNA was discovered, which ultimately led to a revolution in medicine and criminal forensic investigations. A vaccine for polio brought this dreaded disease under control. The space race between the US and the USSR was in full swing by the end of the decade. The Interstate Highway System, the largest public works project in history, was created in the 1950s, just in time to support the explosion in car ownership. And passenger railroads experienced a steep decline as Americans heeded the call to "see the USA in your Chevrolet."

Alaska and Hawaii became the 49th and 50th States in the Union, and their stars were added to our flag. The newly-admitted states became even more popular with tourists from the lower 48. Cuba, however, ceased to be a vacation destination for Americans after the Communist takeover. Europe became a prime tourist destination, and by the end of the decade, more Americans were traveling there on airplanes than on cruise ships.

In athletics, Don Larsen pitched a perfect game in the 1956 World Series. Both baseball leagues still had only eight teams, and the Dodgers and Giants moved to the west coast. In football, college teams played only ten games, freshmen weren't allowed to play varsity sports, and the national champion was decided by polls. In professional football, the National Football

League was the only game in town until the American Football League went into business in 1960. In boxing, Rocky Marciano and Floyd Patterson reigned as heavyweight champions for most of the decade.

In literature, J.D. Salinger's *The Catcher in the Rye* was a huge bestseller among high school and college students. *Lolita*, a novel by Vladimir Nabokov, created a firestorm of controversy with its theme of child molestation. In films, Cecil B. DeMille brought us *The Ten Commandments* from on high, Marlon Brando won the Academy Award for Best Actor in *On the Waterfront* ("I coulda been a contender"), and *Ben-Hur* garnered eleven Academy Awards. And as a bonus, the ultra-widescreen Cinerama process was introduced.

Socially, the United States was transformed during the decade. For the first time, a significant number of high school graduates went on to college, many of them through GI benefits. The *Kinsey Reports* about sexual practices in the US was published to shock and outrage. The civil rights movement was underway in earnest. The landmark case of *Brown vs. Board of Education* in 1954 ultimately led to desegregation of the nation's public schools. Demonstrations in the 1950s and early 1960s led to the passage of the Civil Rights Act of 1964 and the Voting Rights Act of 1965.

Hundreds, perhaps thousands, of books have been written about the 1950s and the political, cultural, and historical events of the decade. But few of these books give the reader a real hands-on feel for what it was like to live during that decade, especially as a kid growing up in that period. Since I did grow up in the 1950s, I remember what it was like, including the little nuts and bolts things of daily life that many books overlook in favor of the headline-making events. And that's what this narrative is about.

I promise that this book is *not* a personal memoir, since with the exception of thirty seconds of intensely excruciating terror in October, 1980 (I'll explain this in the End Notes), my life has been so stupefyingly uninteresting that reading about it would put even a hardened insomniac to sleep. So there's no personal stuff in here except where it helps to illustrate daily life in the 1950s.

I hope you enjoy reading about the Fabulous Fifties as much as I did living them and writing about the experience.

CHAPTER 1

WAR – THE AFTERMATH

World War II was THE event of the 1940s, and it is impossible to understand the 1950s without taking into account the effects of the war on that decade. The war in Europe began in 1939 with the German invasion of Poland. The war in Asia began earlier, in 1937, with the Japanese invasion of China. Although the United States gave material support to our allies, we were not officially at war until the Japanese attacked Hawaii on December 7, 1941, resulting in almost 4,000 American casualties on "a day which will live in infamy" (President Franklin D. Roosevelt in a speech to Congress on December 8, 1941). On December 11, 1941, Germany and Italy, allies of Japan, declared war on the United States.

The war in Europe ended in May 1945 when Germany surrendered. The Japanese surrendered in August 1945 after having US atomic bombs dropped on two of their major cities. The world breathed a huge sigh of relief and started mourning the dead and rebuilding shattered countries. And there were a lot of dead to mourn. Worldwide an estimated 70 million people died because of the war, making WWII the deadliest war ever. More than 400,000 Americans died of the 16,000,000 men and women who served in the military during the war, and almost 700,000 were wounded, many of them crippled or maimed for life. In American history, only the Civil War produced more casualties.

World War II had profound effects on the United States and its people. Unlike other wars or military actions the US has been involved in since 1945, civilians could not simply go about their business and ignore the war or its effects. Millions of men were drafted into military service, resulting in a shortage of men, so women took jobs in defense plants (the origin of "Rosie the Riveter"), the federal government, and privately owned businesses. Many of these jobs required greater skills than traditional women's jobs like waitresses and clerks. Women also took thousands of jobs in agencies like the USO and the Red Cross. Many women even served in branches of the armed forces, including the WAVES (Navy), WASPS (Army Air Force), and WACS (Army).

Because of demands by the military, many critical items were unavailable or were rationed, such as gasoline; tires; sugar; milk, butter, and cheese; coffee; shoes; and many processed foods. Local rationing boards distributed ration books for each person in a family. Many civilians planted "victory" gardens to raise their own fruits and vegetables.

Due to the heavy casualties, most American families suffered the loss of at least one family member, neighbor, or friend. The Gold Star Mothers, formed in 1918, was a support group for mothers who lost children in the war. The entire country mourned the loss of all five Sullivan brothers when their Navy cruiser was sunk at Guadalcanal in 1942.

World War II was arguably the last war in which Americans overwhelmingly believed that large-scale military action was justified. It was considered a "good" war between forces of right against the totalitarian imperialist governments of Germany and Japan. Because of this, Americans who had served overseas during the war were welcomed home as heroes, often receiving parades in their home towns. Many who had served in the military used the war as a springboard to political careers, including Dwight D. Eisenhower, who was elected President in 1952 and was in office for the remainder of the decade. His successor was John F. Kennedy, also a WWII veteran.

On war's end, the country wasted little time getting back to business – literally. All heavy industry, including automobile, aircraft, and ship manufacturing, had been converted to producing war materiel, but assembly lines quickly retooled for consumer products, and former soldiers were now working again as civilians. By 1950, commerce was booming. And commerce wasn't the only thing that was booming. Former GIs were returning home to their wives or marrying their girlfriends, and the post-war Baby Boom was on. The US birthrate soared from 1946 until 1961, and has never reached the same levels since.

The initial post-war optimism that WWII was the war to end all wars was short-lived, as a new war — the Cold War — commenced almost before the ink was dry on the surrender documents. Our wartime allies, the Soviet Union and the People's Republic of China, were now our enemies, and when the Soviets detonated their own atomic bomb in 1949, the 1950s would begin with a bang, quite literally. As one of the two superpowers emerging from the war, the United States would no longer maintain an isolationist policy, since intervention in foreign affairs and support of foreign governments was thought to be essential to stem the swelling tide of Communism.

When the new decade dawned on January 1, 1950, I was three years and five months old, and this would be my coming of age decade, as it would be for several million other Baby Boomers.

Now we've set the stage.

CHAPTER 2

The Family

During most of the 1950s, my family (father, mother, grandmother, my sister Janis [a year younger than me], and me) lived in a tiny cracker box of a house in a suburb of Atlanta. Like many of the tract houses built in the years immediately following the war, the house had two bedrooms, one bathroom, a screened-in porch which the previous owners had enclosed as a third bedroom (a common practice), no air conditioning, and only a furnace in a floor grate for heat. It was cramped, but it was okay until sisters #2 (Jean) and #3 (Susan) came along. My grandmother died before my youngest sister was born, but it was still very crowded for many years. And that's enough of the memoir stuff for now. This isn't about me, it's about life in the 1950s.

Families were generally bigger in the Fifties than they are today. I can't document that, but I knew a lot of kids who had three or four siblings, and I don't know many people today who have more than two or three kids. It also seems like people married at a younger age then, often right out of high school.

One reason for the larger families in the Fifties was the lack of contraception devices and the virtual absence of abortions. Birth control pills, intrauterine devices, and implants didn't exist then. Condoms existed, but based on the high birth rate, they apparently weren't used much. And there was little demand for birth control in the 1950s. Returning GIs, airmen, sailors, and marines were marrying and wanted to start their families.

Abortions were almost unheard of. Although federal laws did not prohibit abortions, almost all states did. A woman who wanted an abortion basically had two options: go abroad to a country that allowed them or have an illegal and dangerous "back alley" abortion that often resulted in the mother's death or serious injury. It wasn't until 1973 in the landmark Roe v. Wade decision by the US Supreme Court that state laws prohibiting abortion were struck down.

The social mores were very different than they are today. Kids almost always had two parents. A single woman who got pregnant was scandalized, and her children had to live under the stigma of being illegitimate. Unmarried girls who got pregnant were often sent away to live with out-of-town relatives until the baby was born, and the baby would be put up for adoption or sent to an orphanage. Pregnant teenagers were sometimes disowned by their parents. Many big cities had Florence Crittenton homes for unwed mothers, where women, usually teenagers, could go for shelter and prenatal care. Only a few of these homes are still in operation today. Divorce was almost as scandalous as unwed pregnancy, with divorcées being looked at as shameful, disreputable women. None of these taboos applied to men, of course.

Family life was in some ways simpler and less hectic in the Fifties than it is today. Since cities were much smaller then, commute times were shorter than today, so working fathers were usually home by 5:30 in the afternoon. When my dad got home from work, we all had dinner together. Meals were real sit-down family affairs, not the quick grab-a-bite-on-the-run things they often are today. My mother got up in the morning long before the rest of us did and started making biscuits from scratch and frying sausage or bacon and eggs ("It ain't breakfast unless a pig died!"). Pillsbury made refrigerated canned biscuits that weren't bad, but our mom insisted on making them from scratch every morning, even though it was a lot of work. Weekday lunches were at school, but dinner was a sit-down time to talk about the day and fill up with our mom's wonderful home cooking. There weren't many so called convenience foods then, so meals were made almost entirely from scratch, a very time-consuming process.

In the South, it was common for unmarried women to have a "hope chest" made of wood in which they collected items to be used in their marriage. Our mom had a big cedar hope chest filled with china, sterling silverware and serving pieces, and expensive linen tablecloths and napkins. These were only used for special occasions, so we seldom saw them. For most meals, we used cheaper steel tableware and ceramic plates. Silver tarnished, so our mother would occasionally take the silverware from the velvet-padded case and polish it, which was quite a job requiring silver polish and a good bit of elbow grease. When she set the table for Thanksgiving and Christmas or when we had company, it looked so impressive with the linen tablecloth and napkins; china plates, cups, and saucers; and the shiny silverware and serving bowls. For a few hours, we felt like rich people, then all the stuff got washed, dried, and put away in the hope chest.

Once in a while, we gave my mom a break and had TV dinners. These were frozen dinners in aluminum trays that were introduced in the early 1950s. You had to stick them in a gas or electric oven for a long time to heat them up. TV dinners wouldn't win any culinary awards, but they were easy to fix, and we enjoyed the novelty of them.

Parents of Baby Boomers had lived through the Great Depression of the 1930s, and many of them remembered having less-than-full bellies at times. They were therefore determined that their kids would never be hungry. That worked in kids' favor, since they fed us well and often, but we were reminded regularly that they had grown up hungry and that we ungrateful little wretches should never waste a single morsel of food. Protestant moms rivaled Jewish mothers in their ability to lay a heavy guilt trip on kids. They would go into a pathetic spiel about the starving kids in India and how we would mail our leftovers overseas except that they would spoil before they got halfway to Bombay. And then a miracle happened that spared us from guilty consciences about wasting food that kids in India needed: Tupperware was invented, and leftovers could be burped and stored forever in airtight plastic containers in the refrigerator. Well, maybe not forever, but long enough.

After each meal, there was the considerable task of washing and drying the dishes and silverware. Automatic dishwashers existed in the 1950s, but they were used mostly in restaurants. Most people couldn't afford them, and most kitchens were too small to accommodate them anyway. Washing clothes also consumed a lot of time. Automatic washers were popular in the 1950s, and most families had them, but clothes dryers didn't become common until later. So we had this marvelous device called a clothesline, where three or four wires stretched between two steel poles with cross pieces. Clothes were hung over the wires and kept from blowing away with wooden clothes pins. If it was raining, you did the best you could to dry the clothes inside the house. As archaic as clothes lines now seem, there was nothing fresher or softer than clothes that were air-dried in the sun. Ironically, as environmentally "green" as clotheslines are, some suburban neighborhoods today ban them as being eyesores.

Washing and drying clothes was just the beginning. In those days before wash-and-wear wrinkle-free clothes, the dried clothes had to be ironed, a tedious process that involved running a heavy, hot iron over them. If the iron was a little too hot or you didn't keep it moving fast enough, it burned a hole in your clothes. And it wasn't just clothes, practically everything got ironed, including bed-sheets and table cloths. Our mothers spent a lot of thankless hours putting clean unwrinkled clothes on us.

If a mother didn't have time to do the washing, drying, and ironing, she could send out the clothes to a laundry. Laundry trucks came through neighborhoods on their routes, and they would pick up your clothes once or twice a week, then deliver them to you ready-to-wear in a couple of days. For most families, however, this was an expensive luxury. Our mom sometimes sent out my dad's dress shirts, since they had to be starched and creased just so. Laundries also did dry cleaning for clothes that weren't supposed to be washed, like jackets and coats or clothes made from delicate fabrics like silk.

Families sometimes ate out at a restaurant, but this was an occasional treat. Think of almost any well known restaurant chain. Very few of them existed in the 1950s. Most restaurants were one-of-a-kind or part of small local chains. In the South, we had Krystal hamburgers. Their little hamburgers served on steamed buns were the best in the world and cost only five cents (later in the decade they went up to a dime, a shocking reminder of inflation). Krystal, the southern equivalent of White Castle, still has the tastiest and most addicting hamburgers in the world in my opinion. They had little competition in the 1950s, since McDonald's and Burger King wouldn't appear on stage until the next decade. For purely local dining, Atlanta had the Varsity, advertised as the World's Largest Drive-In Restaurant. Generations of Atlantans feasted on the Varsity's chili dogs and fries (and still do). You could eat inside or pull your car into the drive-in area and be waited on by car hops, who were famous for their flamboyant costumes. Located next to Georgia Tech, the Varsity was far more popular than the school's dining hall with Tech students, but non-students loved it too.

The microscopic size of our house didn't bother us too much, since we had never lived in a bigger place, and we kids didn't mind sharing small bedrooms together. The real hardship was having as many as six people living in a house with only one bathroom. Our mom at least had a plan for the mornings, and she executed the plan like a precision railroad timetable. Each of us had our assigned time, and if you missed it, you were up the creek. My sister Janis was always last because besides whatever the heck else she did in there, she finished up by emptying a couple of cans of hairspray into her big bouffant hairdo. If you don't know what a bouffant is, send me some money and I'll mail you a picture of her then.

I don't know why it takes females so long in the bathroom, but they've all apparently sworn to never divulge the answer. Ask a woman the big question and they clam up or look at you like you're from Mars. Even my wife won't tell me. Whatever. There were four females in our house, and some days they spent so much time in the bathroom, my bladder came dangerously close to exploding. Outside the kitchen were some steps going down to the back yard. Our mom had a flowering shrub of some kind that she had planted when we moved into the house, and she gave it all the TLC it needed. Unfortunately, the hedge never did well, despite getting plenty of sunshine and fertilizer. After I grew up and moved out, the hedge had a miraculous recovery and flourished for many years. I don't know if my mom ever figured it out, and I never asked. At least living in a house with four females taught me to put the toilet seat down. That lesson has served me well in marriage.

Church was an important part of our lives. They don't call the South the Bible Belt for no reason. As Southern Baptists, our family attended Sunday School and church services on Sunday morning, and the weekly prayer meeting was on Wednesday night. Revivals were held every year or two. By the 1950s, most ministers were seminary-educated, and their sermons were usually thoughtful and inspiring, but occasionally we would get an old-time fire and brimstone preacher at a revival or a funeral, and we would leave scared to death that Satan was lurking around every corner ready to snatch our souls. In the 1950s, there weren't many mega-churches with several thousand members like today. Most churches were smaller, with no more than a few hundred members, and people were close to each other. If a family had a financial problem, the church members would help. The bigger, more structured churches today seem more like corporations sometimes. It's just not the same atmosphere now.

In Atlanta, there were two newspapers, both owned by the same company, and some people read the morning paper, while others read the afternoon paper. In the suburbs, you knew who subscribed to the newspaper, because there was always a separate newspaper box on the post with the mailbox. My parents read the afternoon edition after we had dinner. Before TV news shows existed, daily newspapers were the main source for news, weather, sports, and the most important section – the comic strips, especially after Charles Schulz' *Peanuts* debuted in October 1950. With newspaper readership declining so much in the last few decades, it's hard to realize today how important newspapers were fifty or sixty years ago. Besides the news and editorials, there was a huge classified ads section. If you were looking for a job or you wanted to buy or sell anything, this was the place to go. And people advertised literally everything: cars, jewelry, lawn mowers, pets, cameras, airline tickets (you could sell them in those days), you name it. With all the online media today, classified ads have practically disappeared, along with a big chunk of a newspaper's revenue.

One part of the newspaper that appealed to adults for reasons unfathomable to me was the Society section. The Sunday newspaper had page after page of news about all the debutante balls and which young ladies were having their "coming out" parties, and where the newlywed Mr. and Mrs. so-and-so were honeymooning. And pictures of all the society matrons attending the Metropolitan Opera's annual performances in Atlanta, wearing their mink coats in the sweltering heat of May. I still don't have a clue why this was so fascinating to our middle-class parents, unless it was a life they secretly aspired to.

After the newspaper was read, we gathered around the TV set. TV sets were expensive, so most families had only one, and the family sitting in front of the TV was the 1950s version of the family sitting around the radio in earlier decades, except that you were looking at the TV instead of each other. With only one TV in most homes and three channels to choose from, there was a lot of disagreement over which show to watch. Parents almost always won this argument. I can still remember my father watching boxing matches every Friday night on the *Gillette Cavalcade of Sports*, and I can still whistle the lively Gillette *Look Sharp/Be Sharp* theme music. Our grandmother lived with us, and she watched out for my sister Janis and me. *The Adventures of Rin Tin Tin* was one of our favorite shows, so it was one of her favorite shows. Grandmothers could be so sweet.

Television was not the only nighttime entertainment for families, and in any case, many homes did not have a TV set until the mid-1950s or later. Board games were very popular, and kids played these with other kids or with their parents. For younger kids, games that depended mostly on luck like *Chutes and Ladders* and *Sorry!* were popular. For older kids and their parents, Monopoly was a popular game. Our family's favorite game was *Go to the Head of the Class*, a quiz game for kids and adults, with the questions getting harder depending on the age of the player. Checkers, backgammon, and chess were old games that were still popular in the Fifties, as were card games like *Old Maid* and *Go Fish*.

Besides newspapers, magazines were extremely popular in the 1950s. With their slick pages and gorgeous color photography, magazines like *Life*, *Look*, and *Saturday Evening Post* were enormously popular, and millions of Americans subscribed to them. The beloved artist Norman Rockwell rose to fame largely based on his cover illustrations for *Saturday Evening Post*. Like newspapers, however, magazine sales began to suffer during the Fifties as Americans turned to television, and advertisers followed suit.

Life in the 1950s family was a lot different than it is today. Your parents were not your friends, they were your parents, and they took the responsibility seriously. They were not remotely like the idiotic, syrupy parents in TV shows like *Leave it to Beaver*, *Father Knows Best*, and *Ozzie and Harriet*, where the kids ran roughshod over the grown-ups. It made for good TV, with kids cheering on their heroic peers each week as they outwitted their clueless parents, but in real life, parents were judge, jury, and executioner, and justice was swift and merciless. And there were no appellate courts or last-minute stays of execution. When you earned a spanking, you got it. For lesser offenses, you might get restricted for a few days, but spankings were the preferred punishments. Mothers seldom administered the spanking; that was the father's role. I can still remember shaking in my boots when my mom uttered those blood-curdling words: "Just wait till your father gets home." And it didn't matter if your father traveled and wouldn't be home for a week. There was no statute of limitations that would get you off the hook.

I still remember one incident when I was twelve years old. I had gotten a .22 caliber rifle (a Marlin Model 57 lever action, a really sweet rifle) for my birthday. You couldn't discharge firearms in our suburban neighborhood of course, but I was on the back steps just loading it and unloading it when the rifle accidentally discharged and a bullet went into the wall. I heard my mother scream, and I ran inside to the kitchen, where plaster dust was everywhere (walls were plaster then, not the sheetrock drywall that would come later). The bullet had grazed the plaster and made a very noticeable crater. Fortunately for me, the crater was behind the refrigerator and wasn't very noticeable, especially with the stack of old newspapers on top. My mom calmed down, cleaned things up, and sat me down to explain that if my dad ever found out what happened, he would kill me instantly and without remorse. Therefore, she said, as long as he's alive, we'll keep this refrigerator so he never sees the wall behind it. My father died thirty-two years later, and my mom kept that refrigerator going with duct tape and baling wire. I contributed by praying for the refrigerator's continued health. My dad must have wondered why my mom was so attached to the refrigerator, but he never said anything, and since he was a bit of a cheapskate, it was okay with him to not have to buy a new refrigerator. My mom got a ton of points for that, and afterwards, I upgraded her birthday present considerably from the usual soap-on-a-rope or chocolate-covered cherries. After my dad died, I bought her a new refrigerator, a deluxe model with all the frills. It was worth every penny.

Disciplinarians that they were, our parents were probably a lot easier on us than their parents were on them. *Baby and Child Care*, by Dr. Benjamin Spock, had been published in 1946, and it undoubtedly had an influence on Baby Boomer parents, with its emphasis on being flexible and affectionate with kids, rather than the traditional "spare the rod, spoil the child" approach. Unfortunately for kids, few teachers subscribed to Dr. Spock's enlightened theories, so we were at their mercy for several hours a day. Parents and teachers did have one thing in common though. When asked by a hapless kid why they were being told to do something, the answer was always "Because I said so."

Kids were a sickly lot in the Fifties. You couldn't get past the second grade without getting measles, mumps, and chickenpox. There were even two kinds of measles – the three-day variety and German Measles – and kids usually got both of them. Pink-eye (Conjunctivitis) was common and could affect a whole school. There were no vaccines for these diseases in those days, but they weren't usually too serious, and kids got to stay out of school for a few days and be pampered by their mothers. Kids did get vaccinated for smallpox, diphtheria, and whooping cough before they started first grade, since the schools required it.

The "big one" that parents feared most was polio, also known as infantile paralysis. The "iron lung" respirator was a symbol for this dread disease that had no vaccine and no cure. Caused by a virus, the disease crippled or killed tens of thousands of kids and young adults in the US. By 1952, the disease was epidemic, with almost 60,000 cases reported that year. Since most infections occurred in summers, many parents were reluctant to let their kids play outside until cooler weather came. And then, just like that, the threat was gone. The first effective and safe injectable vaccine was developed by Jonas Salk, and by the late 1950s, many kids were being vaccinated at their doctors and public health centers. The real breakthrough came in the early 1960s when Albert Sabin developed an oral vaccine. By the mid-1960s, entire communities were lining up at their local schools on "Polio Day" to take a little sugar cube holding a drop of the vaccine. Within the space of a few years, polio was virtually eradicated in the United States, and both parents and kids breathed a huge collective sigh of relief. It's hard to imagine today, almost fifty years later, what terror a tiny virus held for people then.

In the Fifties, a few doctors still made house calls, but this practice was fading out fast. Parents were now used to going to a doctor's office for themselves and their kids. There were some practicing pediatricians, but many kids went to the same general practitioners that their parents went to. The early Fifties were a really miserable time for kids whose parents took them to the doctor. Antibiotics were the new wonder drug, and doctors went wild using them. If you were dragged to the doctor with a runny nose, you got a shot of penicillin. If you had a hangnail, you got a shot of penicillin. Drug companies must have gotten filthy rich from all those shots. Another racket was the tonsillitis scam. The first time a kid over five years old with a sore throat was taken to the doctor, the doctor informed the parents that their kid's infected tonsils were spewing germs all over their body and the kid could die if they weren't removed. So the poor kid was sent to a surgeon, who removed his tonsils. Surgeons must have made millions taking out tonsils in the 1950s. I was six years old and my sister Janis was five when our parents took us to the family doctor with sore throats. We got penicillin and were sent to a surgeon, who said our tonsils had to go. My sister Janis was too ignorant to know that meant having razor-sharp knives stuck down her throat. I, however, was in the first grade and had heard all the horror stories from kids who had already had their tonsils ripped out, so I knew there was an overwhelming likelihood the surgeon would accidentally drop my tonsils down my throat and I would choke to death on them. I raised such a fuss that my parents let me off the hook, but Janis went ahead with it, and I had to watch her eat ice cream for a week, the reward for having her tonsils out. That was almost sixty years ago, and she still raves about that ice cream. I asked my mom a few years ago if she would buy me a gallon of my favorite ice cream if I would have my tonsils out now. She said no, I had my chance and blew it.

Mothers had strange ideas about preventative medicine in those days. There was one barbaric practice in particular that still grosses me out. During the winter months, we had to submit to taking a daily teaspoon of cod liver oil. Think about it. They take a cold, dead, smelly fish, cut out its liver, and squeeze the oil and God only knows what else out of it. Then they put this vile stuff in a bottle, and with some ingenious marketing they convince parents that the stuff is good for their kids. So we held our noses and swallowed the stuff, followed by a big slug of orange juice or Hi-C, a juice drink made from oranges and citric acid (not bad, actually – we loved it). We always wondered why if cod liver oil was so good for you, grown-ups never took it. Cod liver oil is one of those childhood memories that's best forgotten.

Mental illness was an issue that no one wanted to talk about. I guess that's still true today, although we've come a long way from the barbaric ways of treating the mentally ill only a few decades ago. In 1837, the Georgia legislature passed a bill calling for the creation of a "State Lunatic, Idiot, and Epileptic Asylum" to be located in Milledgeville, then the state capital. The facility opened in 1842. By the end of the 1950s, Central State Hospital, as it was later named, had almost 12,000 patients and was the largest mental hospital in the United States. During the 1960s, the state began to decentralize mental health treatment by opening regional psychiatric hospitals and community mental health programs throughout the state. But when I was a kid, if you were nuts, you went to Central State Hospital in Milledgeville. When we said someone "should be in Milledgeville," everyone knew what we meant. I guess it's a good sign today that that isn't the case any more. Nowadays, most kids in Georgia have never heard of Milledgeville, and if they have, they think of a small town near Lake Oconee, a popular lake an hour's drive east of Atlanta. In the late 1950s, an aunt of mine who had suffered through years of mental and physical cruelty from living with an abusive alcoholic husband went meshuga and was admitted to Central State. They treated her with electroshock therapy, which is a technical term for running big jolts of electricity through her brain repeatedly until she forget what was troubling her. Unfortunately the treatment was not very selective, so she lost a lot of good memories as well as the bad. Fortunately there are more subtle means available today, including medicines that treat brain disorders.

Family vacations were always the highlight of the year. With a nine-month school year, we and every other family with school-age kids had to go on vacation during June, July, or August (school always ended a few days after Memorial Day and started the day after Labor Day). Like many families, we headed for Florida, usually Jacksonville Beach, but once we went all the way to Miami. A lot of people wouldn't go all the way to Miami, because it was a long drive in an un-air conditioned car over congested two-lane roads. Interstate Highways didn't exist then. We were fortunate, however, since my dad worked for a railroad and we could travel for free in comfort and have great meals in the dining car.

One event that our whole family looked forward to was the Southeastern Fair that was held each fall at the Lakewood

Fairgrounds on the south side of Atlanta. Janis and I loved the rides, the games, and pigging out on cotton candy, candied apples, and popcorn. Our favorite ride was the giant carousel that was a permanent fixture at the fairgrounds. Our favorite ride would have been the Greyhound, a wooden roller coaster built in 1915, but our mom would not let us ride it, saying that it was too old and rickety and that it would fall down one day. She was half right. In the sequel to *Smokey and the Bandit*, the roller coaster was blown up in a spectacular scene at the movie's end.

Family reunions were always fun outings. Since families were generally bigger then, reunions meant a lot of people. Everyone brought pot luck, and the food was great, although some of my aunts had weird ideas about food and insisted on bringing inedible crap like broccoli and chicken gizzards, which our mothers made us eat so we didn't embarrass our aunts. The real treat for kids was making homemade ice cream, which was far better than any store-bought ice cream. It *should* be better, since it took so much work. All the ingredients were put into a metal can and the can was dropped into a big wooden pail, then a hand crank was attached. The area between the pail and the can was filled with a mixture of crushed ice and rock salt. Then it was the kids' turn to crank for a half-hour or so. The older kids knew that the crank got harder to turn as time went on, so they always volunteered to crank first. The younger kids soon learned this trick, however, and they weren't so eager to volunteer the next time. I can still remember cranking an ice cream churn until my arm was about to fall off, but the freezing cold ice cream was worth it. And the kid who churned the most got the biggest reward – to lick the ice cream off the dasher when it was removed from the can.

Between reunions, we visited my aunts and uncles, and in most cases that also meant my cousins, who we only saw every few weeks and who we loved to play with. More often than not, however, our aunts and uncles came to our house, since our grandmother lived with us from the end of WWII until she died in 1956. My sister Janis and I were envied by our cousins, since we had grandma all the time. Grandma's kids, including my mother, nicknamed her "Bruin" because she was a bear to grow up with (my mother's words, not mine!), but she was a lamb with us, and Janis and I fought to see who got to sleep with her at night.

Grandma loved television. Not even having radio until she was in her forties, she was enthralled with TV. Her favorite show was *The Adventures of Rin Tin Tin*, a series about a young orphan boy and his dog who lived on a US cavalry outpost in the west in the 19th century. She never missed it, and even our mom and dad didn't dare outvote her on which show we watched when it was on.

Television was, as I mentioned, a transforming experience for Americans, but I'll cover that more in Chapter 5. Television did give me the chance to get revenge on my sister Janis for the tonsillectomy debacle. One of the big Saturday morning network shows was the *Howdy Doody Show*, which featured "Buffalo Bob" Smith as host with his puppet sidekick Howdy Doody. (Trivia tidbit: Clarabell the Clown was originally played by Bob Keeshan, who eventually left the show and became Captain Kangaroo.) *Howdy Doody* was so popular that many local TV stations had their own weekday afternoon imitations. In Atlanta, it was the *Woody Willow Show* on WSB-TV. About the most exciting thing a kid could do was to be in the "peanut gallery" and cheer Woody on in his never-ending battle against the bad guys. When my cousin Elaine turned eight years old, her mother got tickets and invited our cousin Suzanne and me to be on the Woody Willow show for her birthday. Janis couldn't go, because you had to be at least six years old to be on the show. The three of us had a great time in the peanut gallery singing "Hail, hail, the gang's all here, it's time for Woody Willow...", but Janis was devastated and never recovered from the crushing disappointment. Unfortunately, there was no way to record TV shows in those days, or I would send her a video of the show every year for her birthday. Payback is sooooo sweet!

Most mothers were housewives. Another word, probably more accurate, was "homemakers." Some women were in the job force, but once the kids came along, mothers were expected to stay home and be with their kids. It was a full-time job too. Kids took a lot of a mother's time, and babies required even more of a mother's time and energy. For one thing, disposable diapers didn't exist in the 1950s. Diapers were made of cotton cloth, and when a baby's diaper was changed, the poopy diaper went into a big diaper pail until the next washing. Since a baby goes through an estimated 6,000 diaper changes, that's a lot of poop and a lot of washing until a kid is potty trained. By the early 1960s, disposable diapers such as Pampers began replacing the washable ones, which saved mothers a lot of time and drudgery, but now we have landfills full of the things. At least the poop is biodegradable.

There were no soccer moms in the Fifties, since soccer was virtually unknown in the US in those days. And in any case, soccer players were looked on as wimpy guys who couldn't play a real sport like football or baseball. If moms did carry their kids anywhere, it was probably to Little League baseball or to a Scout meeting. And station wagons were the norm for large families. At the beginning of the decade, most families had only one car, but by the end of the decade, with pressure on mothers to haul their kids around, more and more families had two cars, and builders were pushing new homes with two-car garages or carports.

Mail was a big deal in the Fifties, much more so than today. Long distance phone calls were very expensive, and mail was the only inexpensive way to stay in touch with friends and relatives who lived out of town. Even so, there was surface mail and airmail, and if you wanted a letter to go by airmail, it cost a good bit more. There was no such thing as a fax machine, nor were FedEx or UPS in existence, so documents and packages had to go through the USPS. Mail order was used for buying everything from A to Z, including even firearms (yes, firearms, until President John F. Kennedy was assassinated in 1963 by Lee Harvey Oswald, using a rifle bought by mail order).

One quaint custom that disappeared several decades ago was the regular visits by the "policy man." Companies like Life of Virginia and Metropolitan Life sold life insurance policies through door-to-door salesmen. These policies were small, typically only a few hundred dollars, and were intended to be enough to pay funeral expenses for the insured person. What was unique about them was that policy men sold the policies by walking through neighborhoods selling them and coming back once or twice a month to collect the premiums, which were usually no more than a dollar or so a month. Families actually looked forward to the policy man's visit, since he knew everyone in the neighborhood and would share all the latest gossip. A policy man was like an old family friend, since he knew everyone in your family, and you always got a birthday card from him.

Insurance wasn't the only thing that was sold door-to-door. The Fuller Brush Company salesmen sold brushes, mops, brooms, and cleaning products. By the 1950s, they were a cultural icon, inspiring jokes, movies, and even songs. Avon Products sold cosmetics through its force of traveling saleswomen, one of the few products sold door-to-door by women. "Avon calling" was one of the best-known catchphrases of the era. Other products sold door-to-door included encyclopedias, Bibles, books, magazines, newspaper subscriptions, vacuum cleaners, candy, cosmetics, perfumes, and a lot more. Unlike policy men, most door-to-door salesmen were strangers, but they usually had a good pitch, and most people were too polite to close the door on them, so we bought a lot of useless stuff just to be nice.

Occasionally, someone would come by the house selling spaces in a punch board. Punch boards were gambling devices used for making a profit or for fundraising. The boards were made of thick cardboard with anywhere from a hundred to several hundred holes. The whole board was covered with foil. You could buy holes, typically for 10, 25, or 50 cents a hole. Once the hole was punched out with a stylus, you saw what numbers you had underneath the foil. Some numbers paid money or prizes, but most numbers were duds. A lot of civic organizations, schools, and churches used punch boards for raising money, but sometimes an individual bought the cards and went through neighborhoods selling the holes. Technically, it was gambling, which was illegal in most states, but most states overlooked it, treating it like Bingo, since the stakes were usually pretty low. Punch boards lost their popularity after the 1950s, although they're still used in a few places for fundraising.

The 1950s was a good decade for families and family life, arguably kindler and gentler than succeeding decades. It was the heyday of the so called nuclear family, where a father and a mother lived together and raised their children. In the post-war 1950s, the idea that men would be the primary bread-winners and women would stay home and raise the children was generally accepted. With subsequent increasing divorce rates, later decades would see the gradual breakup of this ideal family situation, as many families included children from previous marriages, and single parenthood became increasingly more common. Feminist movements also contributed to the idea that women had the same social and economic rights as men.

CHAPTER 3

Kids Only

The 1950s was a pretty good decade for kids. It was a less complicated and less structured time, that's for sure. We didn't have most of the things that kids today take for granted, like iPods, cell phones, video games, and home computers, but since we had no concept of such futuristic things, we didn't miss them. It was a safer time for kids back then, and few parents worried much about the adult predators we fear so much today, although every kid was regularly warned to not take candy from strangers. There was some organized play, such as Little League baseball, but mostly the neighborhood kids just got together and played cowboys and Indians or had a pickup game of football or softball, depending on the season. More often than not, our mothers were home, although during the decade, more and more women went off to jobs.

All kids love toys, and Baby Boomers were no exception. Regarding toys, there were fewer government regulations in those days, and most of the toys we played with would probably be banned today. Many toys had small or sharp pieces that could be swallowed, resulting in choking or slicing up your insides, and we probably chewed enough lead paint to supply an ammunition factory. It's a wonder that any of us survived or that our kids weren't born with two heads or other mutations.

There were plenty of innovative toys, and they were inexpensive, since the Japanese industries were rebuilding and flooding the US with cheap products of all kinds. They weren't only cheap to buy, they were so cheaply made that they often fell apart almost as soon as you started playing with them. The quality was so poor that the phrase "Made in Japan" became synonymous with anything of poor quality. This eventually changed of course, but in the 1950s, Japanese imports were just plain crappy, and now-familiar names like Toyota and Nikon were still unknown to us.

The biggest hit of the decade was not, strictly speaking, a toy: the Hula Hoop. Sold by the Wham-O toy company, more than a hundred million of these plastic hoops were bought by Americans in 1957-1958. The craze died as quickly as it began, but for a couple of years the country had to endure the ubiquitous sight of everyone from toddlers to overweight middle-age matrons gyrating their hips to keep the hoop spinning. Following their success with the Hula Hoop, Wham-O introduced the Frisbee, and the world has never been the same.

It's impossible to talk about the Fifties without mentioning the toy that had perhaps the greatest influence on younger kids. Mr. Potato Head was introduced in 1952, and almost overnight this simple toy became the bestselling toy in the United States, and it was the first toy advertised on TV. The concept was absurdly simple. You took a real potato and inserted the hands, feet, ears, mouth, eyes, nose, hat, eyeglasses, a pipe, and felt pieces resembling hair. There was an assortment of pieces for each body part so kids could personalize their own potato. In a brilliant marketing scheme, the manufacturers included an order form in each box for more body parts. In the 1960s, the kits included a plastic body, but with the original Mr. Potato Head, you provided the potato. With millions of kids playing with the things, we probably made millionaires of Idaho potato farmers.

The Barbie Doll was introduced in 1959, so it barely counts as a 1950s toy. Named after designer Ruth Handler's daughter Barbara, it was a phenomenal must-have for girls. Like Mr. Potato Head, Barbies were heavily marketed on TV. Girls who were into realism went for the Betsy Wetsy doll that urinated and wet her diaper after water was poured into her mouth. Another company sued the manufacturer for patent infringements, but a judge ruled that drinking and urinating are natural movements and cannot be patented. Makes sense to me, but hey, I was a boy, and I didn't play with dolls, so who cares.

My favorite toy, if you can call it one, was an Erector Set, a now legendary set of metal parts that you bolted together to make just about anything from bridges to walking robots. The more expensive sets came with gears and an electric motor to make machines that would do most anything, dependent only on a kid's imagination. Erector sets were often the next step up from Tinker Toys, which used wooden dowels and connecting pieces to build things. For an inventive kid (usually boys, but not always), they were great outlets for the imagination. I don't know if anyone has ever done a study, but my guess is that a high percentage of Baby Boomers who became engineers had Erector Sets when they were kids. I did. Today's kids have a similar creative outlet in Legos.

Electric trains were extremely popular with both boys and their fathers. For my sixth birthday, my parents gave me a Lionel train set with the tracks mounted on a big sheet of plywood. The train was the O-gauge, which was a fairly large size that was suitable for younger kids. The smaller, more detailed HO-gauge was just getting popular for serious enthusiasts who wanted to build large, realistic layouts. A few years later, after I had stopped playing with it, my parents gave the train to a co-worker for his son's Christmas. It seemed like a nice thing to do at the time, but that train set is worth a fortune today to collectors.

With the United States and the Soviet Union locked in a titanic struggle for supremacy, science was heavily emphasized in school and by parents. Most kids had a chemistry set. Chemistry sets were always fun, especially when you produced stuff that stank up the house or created some deadly concoction that would eat through your sisters' clothes. The chemistry sets themselves had mostly harmless chemicals, so when you needed acids or bases, you used household stuff like vinegar or bleach. But the really bright kids knew that a cornucopia of serious chemicals was just down the street at the local pharmacy. For a dollar or two, you could acquire all the necessary stuff to create just about anything short of an atom bomb, and some years later, some whiz kid almost did that by extracting radium from old smoke detectors.

When the US started launching rockets into space, there was a national craze by kids to get into model rocketry. You could buy kits with air- or water-propelled rockets, and some kits even had rocket motors with a tiny fuel pellet, but these were so lame that they would barely reach a neighbor's house. Unfortunately, enough of them did reach neighbors' houses that parents quickly took our rockets away from us. So it was back to the pharmacy for some sulfur and potassium nitrate, which when mixed with activated charcoal produced gunpowder. I should explain that in the 1950s, pharmacies didn't just dispense manufactured medicines, they also mixed drugs and chemicals together to make customized medicines; thus the large supply of chemicals available at pharmacies. The few pharmacies that still do this are called compounding pharmacies. Anyway, once you made the propellant, you packed the stuff into a metal pipe with a cap on one end, and you had yourself a rocket. Unfortunately, this is also how you make a pipe bomb, so a lot of kids blew themselves up in the name of science. After a while, it got so bad that pharmacies stopped selling sulfur and potassium nitrate to kids. Eventually adults, mainly teachers, organized rocket clubs and developed safer rocketry for students, but by this time, the junior rocketeers who had survived with all their limbs intact had gone on to college and were working for NASA, which was created in 1958.

One indispensable "toy" for inquiring young minds was a microscope. They weren't really toys though. You could do some serious magnification with the better ones, up to 400 times real size. Eventually though, it got kind of boring looking at hairs and diatomaceous earth, whatever the heck that was. Insect parts and flowers were pretty cool, but eventually they got tiresome too. Blood, however, was always fascinating, since it was alive and moving. I tried extracting a few drops from our cocker spaniel, but the bitch bit me, so that ended the quest for animal blood. Getting fresh human blood presented a bit of a challenge too, since I'm too squeamish to draw my own blood, but my sisters' blood was perfectly acceptable, and I only needed a few drops.

As usual, they were completely uncooperative, but a small bribe usually did the trick. A nickel went a long way fifty years ago.

An ultra successful toy for both kids and grownups was the View-Master, a handheld viewer that held stereographic picture disks that you viewed in 3-D. With their own View-Master, a kid could watch cartoons spring to life or see spectacular images of national parks or whatever they fancied, limited only by how many disks the parents would buy. And they bought a lot – an estimated 1.5 billion disks have been sold since View-Masters were introduced at the New York World's Fair in 1939.

On rainy days, many boys (and sometimes their fathers) assembled plastic models. Aircraft were the most popular models, featuring a lot of WWII aircraft plus the newer jet aircraft of the Fifties, but cars and ships were also popular. Revell and Monogram were the biggest manufacturers. Revell made the most accurate and detailed models, while Monogram models were less detailed but had a lot of moving parts like retractable landing gear. You put the things together with plastic cement and then applied decals with the plane's markings. If you were really into accuracy, hobby shops sold brushes and tiny bottles of paint. Models of sailing ships were more of a challenge, since you had to cut many lengths of thread for the rigging, then delicately cement the threads without a blob of cement showing. A kid's father usually had to help with this, and some men liked to build models themselves. If you had a model you were especially proud of, it was back to the hobby shop for a protective plastic display case that kept the dust off.

Illegal drugs weren't a temptation for us because we had no idea they even existed. There was another temptation that was one rung below drugs on the forbidden list, but this one had more of a presence in our lives, and constant vigilance was required to stay on the straight and narrow path. Young boys were warned by their ministers, teachers, and parents to avoid pool halls like the plague. These dens of iniquity were a fast and sure path to the fires of Hell. You remember the scene from the movie *The Music Man* where Robert Preston tells the townspeople "You got trouble with a T, and that rhymes with P, and that stands for Pool"? That was enough to get the people so concerned for their sons' virtue that they spent a fortune on band instruments and uniforms to keep them occupied and away from pool halls. River City may have been a fictional place, but the idea of their sons ending up as pool hustlers worried the daylights out of many parents. Ironically, by the early 1960s, pool halls had cleaned up their act with modern, well lighted, comfortable facilities and were marketing themselves to families, but the stigma never left, and eventually the hustlers came back. A pool hall is, after all, a pool hall.

Unlike pool halls, bowling alleys were able to turn around their unsavory image and thrive during the Fifties. After declining during the Great Depression and World War II, new bowling alleys built in the Fifties were located in suburban neighborhoods and appealed to families as an inexpensive activity that parents and kids alike could enjoy together. Both AMF and Brunswick lanes had new automatic pinsetters which replaced pin boys and speeded up the game, and they had bowling balls of different weights, which made it easier for women and kids to bowl. Bowling alleys recruited in the schools and created junior bowling leagues that were very popular with kids. At three games for a dollar, it was affordable, and lanes were full on Saturday morning with kids' leagues. Another game that kids enjoyed was duckpins, although there weren't as many duckpin alleys as regular bowling alleys. We used to go to Clifton Springs, a few miles away, where the old bowling alley also had several lanes for duckpins. The duckpin balls were smaller than bowling balls, weighing only four pounds and being about the size of a grapefruit. Clifton Springs was an old-timey bowling alley with pin boys, a colorful reminder of what bowling was like before automatic pinsetters.

Pinball machines weren't quite as low class as pool, but many a kid spent their time and their nickels playing the pinball machines in the local drugstore. Some states banned pinball machines as being gambling devices, but they were legal in Georgia, and we loved to play them. Pinball machines were big, heavy machines with real steel balls that rolled around, not like the digital pinball games that are played on a computer or video game machine now.

Kids were a lot more fit in the Fifties, before all the electronic entertainment came along to turn them into couch potatoes. After school, we played outside until it got dark or our mothers called us in for dinner. We played cops and robbers, cowboys and Indians, hide and go seek, kick the can, football, softball, and games we just made up. Basketball was fun, but you had to have a basketball goal. Football was a good game when you had at least 8-10 players, but all of us didn't have footballs, so you had to let the kid who had the ball play, even if he was a whiny little turd who nobody liked. Since you had to let the kid who owned the ball score occasionally, it was an advantage to have him on your team. If he wasn't having fun or if someone hit him too hard, the kid would start crying and take his ball and go home.

All kids had bicycles. They were our modern equivalent of a horse, and your freedom and mobility were assured once you learned to ride a bicycle and took off the training wheels. Girls rode too, but they rode bicycles without a cross bar, since they usually wore dresses and didn't want their underwear to show. We rode everywhere. Once the bicycle training wheels were off, we rode around the neighborhood, to school, to the drugstore, just about anywhere. We clipped playing cards to the bicycle with clothespins so they would make a clacking motorcycle sound when we rode.

American bicycles in those days had fat balloon tires, coaster brakes, and no gearshift. Schwinn was the big name in bicycle manufacturing. Americans who had been based in Great Britain during World War II had gotten used to English bicycles, which were very different, having thinner tires, hand brakes, and gearshifts. As a result, American bicycle companies began making bicycles modeled after the English bicycles. The idea of hand brakes was so radically different, however, that some early models of these bicycles had hybrid brakes, with a hand brake for the front wheel and a coaster brake for the rear wheel. My first "grown-up" bicycle was one of these, and it was a great bicycle, but you learned real quickly to apply the rear coaster break first, or you could go flying over the handlebars, which wasn't a good thing, since no one wore crash helmets then, not even kids.

Downtown Atlanta was a special place for us, but it was too far to walk, and the roads were too busy for parents to let us ride our bicycles. So one of the biggest treats was for our mom to take my sister Janis and me downtown. We rode the bus from our house to the nearby town of Decatur, then took an electric trolley downtown. These trips usually involved lunch at a dime store lunch counter and a movie at one of the downtown movie theaters. There were several dime stores (also called "five and dimes") downtown, including Woolworth's, Kresge's (went on to become Kmart), and W.T. Grant. The lunch counters were the real attraction, with the long countertops and rows of stools, the spiffy waitresses, and the best grilled cheese sandwiches and fries in the world. After lunch, it was time for a movie at one of the downtown theaters such as the Fox, Lowe's Grand (where *Gone With the Wind* premiered in 1939), or the Paramount, which were plush pleasure palaces with nooks and crannies that kids could explore for hours until reined in by their moms. Sadly, both the dime stores and movie theaters disappeared from downtown Atlanta decades ago, victims of increasing suburban sprawl and the rise of suburban shopping malls.

If our mom was on a shopping expedition downtown, that was really a big deal for Janis and me, since it meant a trip to Rich's department store. Rich's was like a dime store on steroids. It was huge, with two buildings located on either side of Forsyth Street in the heart of downtown Atlanta. The buildings were connected by a multi-level glassed-in skybridge. The place was big enough to get lost in, so our mom kept us close. She bought most of our family's clothes at Rich's, many of them in the bargain basement, which really was in the basement. The highlight of a trip to Rich's was to have lunch in the Magnolia Tea Room. It was about the fanciest place we ever ate at as kids. What I remember most was the scrumptious chicken salad and the heavenly pecan pie, washed down with iced tea so sweet it made your teeth ache. As much fun as Rich's was, during the

Christmas season, it was an absolutely magical place for kids. On Thanksgiving night, thousands of families came to watch the lighting of the Great Tree on top of the skybridge connecting the two Rich's buildings. A few days later, our mom would take Janis and me to Rich's to meet Santa Claus and ride the Pink Pig, a miniature monorail that carried kids on a ride through the toy department. It didn't get any better than that for kids.

A lot of kids joined the Boy Scouts and Girl Scouts and their equivalents for younger kids, Cub Scouts, Brownies, and Campfire Girls. Parents encouraged this, believing (correctly) that scouting would help their kids develop character and physical fitness. Scouting also encouraged patriotism and spiritual growth. Many Scout troops were sponsored by local churches, and they worked with churches and civic organizations to raise funds for charity. Millions of city kids learned about the outdoors through hiking, camping, and working on merit badges. During National Scout Week, we proudly wore our uniforms to school. I have very fond memories of my scouting days.

Television had an enormous impact on the nation, as much on kids as grownups. By the mid-1950s, a majority of American households had a TV set. TV was a godsend for harried mothers with a house full of hyperactive kids on a cold or rainy day. Just set them in front of the TV set, and it was like instant hypnosis. The picture was black and white, grainy, and flickered every time an airplane flew over, but nobody cared. Like their parents, kids were enthralled with television in ways that radio could never equal. Kids had their own TV shows on the weekday afternoons and Saturday morning. On weekday afternoons, there were *American Bandstand,* where host Dick Clark brought rock 'n' roll to America's youth, followed by the *Mickey Mouse Club,* which always opened with "The Mickey Mouse March," a tune that millions of Baby Boomers can still hum (ask one!).

Saturday morning was almost entirely devoted to kids' programming. Shows like *Fury* (a boy and his horse), *Sky King* (a cowboy with an airplane and his silly bimbo niece swooping down and nabbing the bad guys, who were dumb enough to stand around until he landed and taxied up), *Howdy Doody* (a freckle-faced marionette), and *The Roy Rogers Show* (Roy and Dale Evans as modern-day cowboys) captured kids' imaginations and kept the streets safe for adults until noon, when kids rushed out to play and turned over control of the TV to their parents. One Saturday morning show that parents encouraged their kids to see was *Mr. Wizard*, where science guru Don Herbert did really nifty science experiments with a young assistant. You could actually do the experiments yourself with household items. An extraordinarily successful show, *Mr. Wizard* aired from 1951-1965.

On weekday mornings, three now legendary TV shows were aimed at preschoolers: *Romper Room*, *Ding Dong School*, and *Captain Kangaroo*. *Romper Room* and *Ding Dong School* were similar shows where the hostesses, "Miss Nancy" and "Miss Frances," respectively, led their group of toddlers in games, exercises, and songs. *Captain Kangaroo*, featuring Captain Kangaroo, Mr. Green Jeans, and a cast of zany regulars, first aired in 1955 and became one of the longest-running shows in TV history. Only *Sesame Street*, which premiered in 1969, ran for a longer time.

There were so many cowboy shows on TV that it had a huge influence on kids, at least young boys. We all wanted to be cowboys, riding the range and going after cattle rustlers, bushwhackers, and other assorted bad guys. All of had our six-guns (toy cap pistols), jeans, cowboy shirts, ten-gallon hats and – most important – cowboy boots. Shoe stores could hardly keep them in stock as the cowboy shows proliferated on TV. After the craze was over and our parents got tired of us clunking around in cowboy boots, we went back to our high-top canvas and rubber Keds and PF Flyers. No Nikes or Reeboks back then.

Some of the kids' TV show commercials were pretty clever, persuading kids to beg their parents to buy the sponsors' products to get a little toy or novelty inside the product. The really clever sponsors had kids send in product box tops or labels plus a small amount of money to get a decoding device so you could read the secret message from the show's hero each week. The cleverest idea, however, was one where you talked your parents into sending a dollar to get a sheet of transparent vinyl that stuck to your TV screen by static electricity. You also got a grease pencil. The idea was that when the show's cartoon hero got in trouble and had to cross a raging river or something, you drew him a bridge or whatever the hero needed to escape from the bad guys. My sister Janis and I got one. We flipped a coin to see who would do the drawing the first week, and I won, but I was having so much fun that she starting yelling and trying to take the pencil away. Getting tired of our noisy squabbling, our dad came over and took the plastic thing and the pencil away, and we never saw them again. Deferred gratification was never one of Janis' strong suits. Somehow the stupid cartoon character made it through without us.

Fireworks had the same allure for kids as they do today. In Georgia in the 1950s, they were legal to sell in some counties, illegal in others. They were illegal in DeKalb County where we lived, but a few feet over the Gwinnett County line a short drive away, there was a huge fireworks stand. There you could buy all the firecrackers, skyrockets, roman candles, M-80s, cherry bombs, sparklers, and any other pyrotechnic stuff you wanted. They had rockets that were probably as advanced as anything the military had then. The best stuff was saved for the Fourth of July and New Year's Eve. Unfortunately, on those days, the local hospital emergency rooms were filled to overflowing with idiots who got burned or blew themselves up. It got so bad that the Georgia legislature banned the sale of fireworks in 1962.

One fireworks product that was very popular with kids were cracker balls. These were little paper balls about a quarter of an inch in diameter filled with a few grains of gunpowder. You threw them against a hard surface and they exploded with a sharp crack and a puff of smoke. They were considered fairly harmless, so most parents would let their kids buy them. One day a kid in my school had just bought a box of them and put them in his back pocket while he went skating. Unfortunately he slipped and fell backward. The whole box of cracker balls went off and blew a big hole in his ass. You had to see it to believe it, and of course the stupid kid went around showing it to everyone after he got out of the emergency room. So no more cracker balls for us, all because of one moron.

Most kids, however, didn't blow themselves up while skating. We didn't need explosives to hurt ourselves, we did a good enough job of that as it was. Roller skates weren't anything like the skates of today. Our skates had four steel wheels set in two side-by-side pairs. A strap around your ankle attached the back of the skate, and the front attached with clamps that slid over the sole of your shoe. You adjusted the clamp with a skate key. (These skates wouldn't work with many shoes today, since the shoe had to have a thick leather sole.) We skated all over the neighborhood. Sidewalks were preferable, but if there were no sidewalks, we skated in the street. All it took was hitting a crack or a joint in the sidewalk to go sprawling, and scraped hands, elbows, and knees were unavoidable. But we were kids, and our moms would clean us off and patch us up with iodine and band-aids. When a pair of skates broke, we would take one of the skates apart and nail the two halves to a 2x4 board, making a crude skateboard.

For boys, at least in the South, getting a rifle was a routine rite of passage. A BB gun like the Daisy "Red Ryder" was for starters, and after a boy proved that he could use it safely without shooting out a window or his eye, he usually got a .22 caliber rifle. Fortunately, we lived on the edge of suburbia, and a mile or so away was a big forest where a friend and I could safely shoot squirrels. And we did shoot safely. Our parents – mothers and fathers – drummed it into us that weapons could injure or kill people. In that period, even very young kids played with toy guns, and we "killed" our friends many times over. But we were taught that real guns could kill, and we never forgot that.

It's hard to believe now, but after I got my .22 rifle for my twelfth birthday in 1958, I regularly walked two miles to a friend's house, where we fired our rifles into a backstop his father had made. That's not remarkable. What is remarkable is that I walked most of the distance along some very busy roads carrying my rifle and no one ever called the police. I doubt if any passing motorists even thought of stopping and calling the police (they would have had to stop and use a pay phone, since cell phones wouldn't come along for another three decades). That's the way it was. You saw a kid with a rifle, you assumed he knew how to use it safely and that he was not a mass murderer.

There were a lot of guns in the post-WWII years, and they were cheap. There were millions of surplus military rifles on the market, and you could get them for a few dollars. There's an old joke from the 1950s: "For sale – WWII French Army rifles, excellent condition, only thrown down once." Many returning WWII veterans got their first hunting rifles for $10 or $15 at military surplus stores, which were everywhere in the Fifties. In most states, you could even buy rifles by mail order. It was also a great time to buy bargain camping equipment, since military surplus stuff was dirt cheap. The United States spent an estimated $288 billion ($3.6 trillion in current dollars) during WWII, and a lot of the hardware we bought came back. Many Boy Scout troops bought enough equipment to last for years.

Boys may have felt like men while they were using their rifles to rid the world of rodents, but they quickly learned not to talk like men. In the 1950s, there was no profanity on TV and very little in the movies. Let your parents hear a four-letter word pop out, and you were in deep doo-doo. This got you a spanking, and your mouth got washed out with soap. Some brands of soap were less objectionable than others, but they all tasted horrible, and puking was almost a relief, since it got rid of the soap taste.

The most popular collectible for boys were baseball cards. It wasn't like today, where you just buy a pack of cards or a whole box of them. Boys in the Fifties bought them one card at a time, with each card being wrapped with a flat piece of bubble gum. The price: one penny. Mickey Mantle, Willie Mays, and Hank Aaron were the most sought-after ones, but for every superstar you got, you got a couple of hundred almost worthless no-name guys. Boys kept their cards in shoe boxes, and trading went on year-round. Some time after I got older and no longer traded the cards, my mother threw them out. I guess it was payback for all the soap-on-a-rope I gave her for Christmas. If I had those cards today, I would be wealthy beyond my wildest dreams.

The cards were precious to us because we loved baseball with a deep passion. In the Fifties, there were only sixteen major league teams, but since New York City had three teams (Yankees, Giants, and Dodgers) and Chicago had two teams (Cubs and White Sox), only thirteen US cities had major league teams. The closest major league team to Atlanta was the Cincinnati Reds (for part of the decade, they were renamed "Redlegs" because of the fear of Communism). Cincinnati was almost 400 miles away, which was a very long drive in those days before Interstate Highways, so very few kids who grew up in Atlanta ever saw a major league baseball game before the Milwaukee Braves moved to Atlanta in 1966. The few kids who had seen a major league game could milk it for years, telling and retelling the story dozens of times to a rapt audience of envious listeners.

Pets were of course very popular in the Fifties, and most families with kids had a dog and/or cat, often several dogs and cats. Most of our dogs and cats were just mutts and alley cats, but some people had registered purebreds. We got our pet dogs and cats from neighbors or the local Humane Society. Kids couldn't have cared less about having registration papers for their dog. Our pets were our friends and we didn't care much about pedigrees. The most popular dogs were Cocker Spaniels, Scottish Terriers, German Shepherds, Labrador Retrievers, Golden Retrievers, Bassett Hounds, Dachshunds, and Poodles. There were a few other breeds, but nothing like the huge number of breeds seen today. If we had ever seen anything like a Bichon Frise, we would have mistaken it for a large rodent and stepped on it. We fed our dogs Ken-L Ration, a canned dog food that isn't made any more. It was pretty smelly, but dogs loved it. Around the end of the decade, a dry dog food called Gravy Train came on the market and was heavily advertised on TV. You added warm water, stirred it up, and it looked like beef stew. At least it looked like beef stew in the commercial. In real life, it looked like crap, and our dog didn't like it, so it was back to the stinky Ken-L Ration.

One pet tradition that would be seriously frowned on today was parents getting their kids baby chickens for Easter. I have no idea how this custom started, and eventually it became unfashionable, since the animals usually died within a few days. Apparently, the chicks that stores sold for Easter were young roosters which are usually killed after birth anyway, so some enterprising poultry producer came up with the idea of dyeing the rooster chicks with food coloring and selling them. They were cute, but many kids mistreated them, and parents got tired of having chicken poop all over the house. When I was about eight years old, Janis and I got two of these little chicks for Easter. We took good care of them, keeping them outside in a homemade chicken coop. They were dyed green and red, and we named them Sonny and Reddy after two TV cartoon characters. They actually flourished and grew for several months till the food coloring was almost worn off and they were beginning to crow. Our parents then suggested that we take them out in the country to where one of our relatives lived. There they would live with the other chickens and have a long, happy life. For several years afterward, every time we went to see our relatives, they would point out Sonny and Reddy, although they looked just like the other chickens to us. Many years later, when Janis and I were in our late-teens, our mom casually remarked that our relatives had killed and eaten Sonny and Reddy a few days after we left them. Parents could be unspeakably cruel at times.

This wasn't my only traumatic chicken incident. My sisters and I were suburban kids. Several aunts and uncles still lived in the country, and our parents thought it would be a good idea for us to spend some time in the country, so for a week every summer, my sister Janis and I lived with Aunt Beatrice, whose two sons were grown and on their own. Aunt Beatrice spoiled us rotten, and we loved it, except for having to use an outhouse, since like many rural people, her house did not have an indoor bathroom. But we were adventurous kids, and the outhouse was just part of the adventure. One afternoon, Aunt Beatrice asked us if we wanted fried chicken for dinner. Of course we said yes, figuring that she would go to the store and get a nice ready-to-cook chicken. Instead, we followed her to the backyard, where she proceeded to grab one of the chickens and chop its head off with a hatchet. With blood still spurting from the chicken's neck, she plucked the feathers off and gutted the chicken. An hour later, the chicken was frying in a skillet. For some reason, none of this bothered Janis, but I couldn't eat anything that night, and I didn't eat chicken for the next five years. I had always just figured Aunt Beatrice kept the chickens in her backyard as pets. It had never dawned on me that she ate them.

In Atlanta, we seldom had snow, so we envied kids in the north who got to throw snowballs, build snowmen, and ride sleds all winter. You couldn't even make a decent snow angel in the light dusting of snow we occasionally got in the winter. Once in a while, however, we got a real snow with an inch or more on the ground. It was great for kids, since schools closed down. Since we didn't have sleds, and I doubt if you could even buy one in Atlanta, we flattened cardboard boxes and rode them down driveways or hills until they got soaked and disintegrated. Since we had little experience with snow, our snowmen were crude but passable. The big treat was snow ice cream. If there was even a half-inch of snow, we were out scooping it into a bowl and making ice cream by mixing milk, sugar, and vanilla with the snow. It was the best ice cream we ever ate, but it was a rare delicacy in the South. Now that I'm grown up, I still enjoy the beauty of seeing snow falling, but it's a pain in the ass to have to deal with icy roads and driveways. Now I know why so many Yankees have moved to the South.

CHAPTER 4

School

The 1950s weren't all fun and games for kids, of course. There was the necessary evil called school. There were no public kindergartens or preschools then, so kids started the first grade at the age of six, unless your parents were wealthy enough to send you to a private kindergarten. In Georgia, there were only two levels of public schools in the 1950s: elementary schools, which included grades 1-7, and high schools, which included grades 8-12. Middle schools didn't come along until several decades later.

Few new schools had been built during the Great Depression or during the wartime 1940s, so many schools dated back to the 1930s. They were sparse to say the least. It was practically unheard of for a school to be air conditioned or have central heat. Cast iron radiators were the norm for heating. If you sat near one, you got char-broiled; if you sat more than a few feet away, you froze and lost all feeling in your extremities.

High schools did have a gymnasium and a football field, usually with a running track around it. The running tracks were often surfaced with cinders or clinker, which were waste products from manufacturing that the schools probably got for free for hauling it away. This was really nasty stuff. It looked okay until you fell and felt hundreds of glass-like shards scraping and puncturing your skin. The stuff took months to work its way out of your skin, and if you were lucky, you didn't get an infection and have to have a limb amputated.

The school atmosphere was very different than it is today. There were no armed security guards or metal detectors. We didn't need them. Our enemies were already inside the school – the principal and the teachers. Don't get me wrong, most teachers were dedicated educators, but they were part of a vast right-wing conspiracy with our parents to make sure we got an education. "Spare the rod, spoil the child" was officially part of the curriculum. Forget the old pictures showing the misbehaving kid wearing a dunce hat sitting on the stool in a corner of the classroom. Mere humiliation would have been fine, but our teachers were seriously into corporal punishment, and parents supported them one hundred percent. Most teachers in the 50s were women, but that didn't keep them from wielding a mean wooden paddle. The most popular model was the size and shape of a cricket bat with the emblem "Ye Olde Board of Education" burned into it. Some paddles even had scientifically-designed holes to increase the paddle velocity to produce maximum pain and suffering. The few teachers who had any qualms about blistering a kid's ass would send the miscreant to the principal's office, where the principal had no such reservations. "Bend" and "over" were the only two words some kids ever heard from the principal, who was like the captain of a ship, with supreme authority over every kid, although mercifully, keelhauling and hanging a kid from the yardarm were not allowed. But a school paddling was just the first step in a cruel two-phase process, since after the paddling, the teacher would call the kid's mother to tell her that her kid had been punished for talking in class, pulling a girl's pigtails, being a Commie sympathizer, or some other crime against humanity. Then the poor kid had to sweat out the rest of the day knowing that his father would finish the job when he got home.

But school wasn't all grim, and kids did actually get an education. Many parents of Baby Boomers had never gone to college, and some had even dropped out of school during the Great Depression of the 1930s to work and help support their families. As a result, parents were determined that their kids would get a good primary education, graduate from a good college, and get a good job. The Cold War with the Soviet Union spurred a competitiveness between the East and West that included education, especially in mathematics and the sciences. When the Soviet Union detonated an atomic bomb in 1949, Americans figured that their spies had stolen our nuclear secrets (they had), but when they orbited their Sputnik satellite in 1957, the United States went ballistic with the sudden realization that simple Slavic peasants had beaten us into space. By the time I started high school in 1959, colleges were already beginning to churn out more math and science teachers, and high schools got serious about science and math, building new science laboratories and buying science and math textbooks that weren't decades old. Georgia, like a number of other states, took advantage of the advent of television to create and operate TV stations aimed at in-school instruction. Prior to this, the most advanced audio-visual media devices used in schools were the filmstrip projector and the 16mm movie projector, both of which were vastly more entertaining than listening to a boring teacher. The more advanced filmstrip projectors had a recorded soundtrack that played on a 33-rpm record player. The record would beep when the teacher was supposed to advance the film to the next picture. In theory this should have worked well, but after the record had been played a few hundred times and dropped on the floor occasionally, it was mostly just muffled, crackly noise, so the teacher would turn it off and just wing it from the printed script. The 16mm movie projectors were preferred by kids, since it was always fun to watch the teacher fumble through the tricky process of threading the film through the projector. The film was guaranteed to break at least once, causing the teacher to mumble a few choice four-letter words, or even better, the film would hang up and begin burning, sending forth clouds of toxic fumes that sent everyone scattering.

In some ways, it was easier to excel in school then than it is now. For one thing, there were fewer distractions and temptations. There were no iPods, video games, cell phones, DVDs, or home computers that kids spend so much time with today. These modern marvels were still decades away. Television, which exploded onto the national scene in the 1950s, was of course, a major distraction, and parents learned quickly that kids needed to do their homework before turning on the TV set.

About temptations: Illegal drugs certainly existed long before the Fifties, but we were blissfully unaware of them. Every high school had one or two boys who were rumored to use marijuana, but these were the ducktail haircut, pegged pants-wearing James Dean wannabes who wore black leather jackets with dozens of zippers (think *Westside Story*). And our mothers told us to stay away from these malignant devils, or we would be doomed to reefer madness the rest of our short, wretched existence. And we did stay away, most of us at least, but those jackets sure were cool. As for heavier drugs, most of us had never heard of them, except for heroin, and everyone knew that was only a big deal "up north." We didn't know about sniffing paint, but the ones of us who built plastic airplane models probably fried parts of our brains with the cement that was used.

Teachers weren't paid very much, I guess because traditionally most teachers were either married women whose husbands were the main bread-winners, or spinsters who had no social life and didn't need much money. But our teachers always dressed professionally. Men teachers wore suits. Women wore dresses and high heels. Pantsuits were unknown, and anything remotely resembling a miniskirt would have gotten the teacher sacked on the spot. Teachers were expected to set a standard in dress and decorum, and for the most part they did.

Since Al Gore had not yet invented the Internet, school kids spent a lot of time in the library. Each school had its own library, but even in a big high school, the library was not very big, so regular trips to the county library were required. Libraries of any kind had strict rules: no talking, no eating, no drinking, no loitering, no having fun. And there was a strict rule that librarians had to be repressed old maids who wore their hair in tight buns and knew how to crack a heavy wooden yardstick over a kid's knuckles if they were unruly or committed the deadly sin of bringing back a book that was overdue. But librarians were keepers of the sacred card file and the mysterious Dewey Decimal System, and that gave them a vaunted status in the community. When teachers assigned a certain book to be read, there was a mad dash by all the kids in her class to be the first one to the school library to check out the one or two copies of the book. If you were too late, you and the other losers stampeded to the county library after school, only to find that a teacher at another school had assigned the same book the day before. So you ended up going to a bookstore and buying an expensive copy of an interminably boring book like *Pride and Prejudice*. Then a couple of weeks later, you had to turn in a book report, where the teacher would mark down your grade for suggesting that Jane Austen should have been tortured and euthanized at an early age. By the way, some teachers did have at least a passable sense of humor, but we now know from DNA testing that English teachers lack the humor gene.

The following year, when English teachers in our county assigned *Sense and Sensibility* by the same Jane Austen, the light went on and we realized that the English teachers were in a lucrative conspiracy with publishers to sell boring books to us. I have no doubt that if the money had been there, the teachers would have had us reading *Tropic of Cancer* or *Peyton Place*. At least we might have enjoyed those.

There was one trick that kids used to get out of reading a long book. *Classics Illustrated* were comic book versions of many classic novels, like The *Three Musketeers*, *Moby Dick*, and *Huckleberry Finn*, and they were illustrated. They even had helpful notes about the author and the novel's setting, so you could read the comic book and crank out a decent book report in an amazingly short time. Unfortunately, teachers figured this out pretty quick and started giving tests on things that weren't in the comic book, and we were found out. I mean *they* were found out, since I never did this myself.

To avoid having to practically live in the library, an encyclopedia was a must for every family with school kids. These were sets of books that weighed a ton and filled an entire bookcase, plus the yearly supplements, and they were expensive. But you really did need them, since they were invaluable sources for information in those pre-Internet days. The two best-known names were *The World Book* and *Encyclopedia Britannica*. Elementary schools actually encouraged parents to buy these by letting company representatives do presentations in the classroom, with the kids taking home the brochures. If the parents mailed back a card, a representative came to your house and made the sales pitch to the parents. My parents were so impressed that they bought the deluxe white set of *The World*

Book. The blue and red versions were exactly the same except for the quality and color of the binding, but the salesman convinced my parents that my self esteem would be permanently bruised if they bought a cheaper binding. It was a practice called "keeping up with the Joneses," an American tradition that kept the economy booming. Actually, our next-door neighbors were the Benefields, and they had already bought the white binding, so my parents had no choice but to follow suit.

I have to admit that in one subject – history - kids in the 1950s had it much easier than today's students. Our history textbooks were old, with American History textbooks ending with the Treaty of Versailles that ended World War I in 1919. All the bellyaching our parents did about surviving the Great Depression of the 1930s went right over us. We didn't study it in school, so it didn't happen. World History textbooks were even worse – or better, from our viewpoint – by ending after Napoleon's defeat at Waterloo. So don't ask me about the Boer War or the Boxer Rebellion – they never happened.

To keep up with current events, elementary school teachers used newspapers a lot. Once a week, we had to bring in a newspaper clipping of a recent story or article about something we thought was important. "Important" had a lot of room for interpretation, so we got a mixed bag of national and international news, sports, financial news, and editorials. I remember one kid bringing in his favorite comic strip, but he got yelled at, so no more comic strips. More enjoyable was the once-a-week event when the teacher passed out our copies of the *Weekly Reader*, a little illustrated news magazine for kids. There were different versions for different grades, so we weren't reading over our head.

Patriotism was very much alive and well in the schools of the 1950s. Every day started with the pledge of allegiance, and no one had any qualms with this. If they had, we would have beaten the Commie crap out of them. If the teacher asked someone to lead the Lord's Prayer, no problem. Our parents and teachers instilled in us a love of God and country that is sadly lacking today to our detriment.

Although the country was booming again a few years after WW II ended, it was impossible for us Baby Boomers to be completely oblivious to the fact that the world had been at war only a few months before we were born. One of the results of the war was a huge national debt, which continued to grow with the onset of the Korean War in 1951. The US government vigorously promoted savings bonds, which grown-ups called war bonds. The smallest denomination was $25, which was the redemption value of the bond after a certain number of years had passed. The $25 bonds cost $17.50. Millions of these bonds were sold through public schools through a savings stamp program. Every student had a book where the stamps were pasted in, and when the book was full, you traded it in for a $25 bond. The idea was to fill at least one book each nine-month school year. So once a week, kids brought their money to school and bought their stamps, which sold for ten cents and twenty-five cents. Buying savings bonds was promoted as a patriotic thing, and kids were strongly urged to buy the stamps each week.

When I said savings bonds were vigorously promoted, I meant it. Even celebrities got in on it. One of the most popular TV shows in the 1950s was *The Lone Ranger*. One day around 1960, Clayton Moore, the actor who played the Lone Ranger, came to my high school to promote savings bonds. To our huge disappointment, neither his horse Silver or his Indian sidekick Tonto, were with him. They drove the Lone Ranger around the football field a few times in a convertible, and that was it. Pretty exciting, yes, but not exactly the "Hi-yo Silver, away!" and off into the sunset that we expected.

One of my pet peeves about school was the use of substitute teachers. I know they were necessary, but many of them didn't have a teaching degree or background and were just doing it to make a few extra bucks, so they were just glorified babysitters. Even worse were the old ones - always women - who had retired from teaching decades earlier. Even though teaching methods had advanced, they were stuck in the 1930s mode. One of them who filled in for one of my teachers who was out sick a lot noticed one day that I was left-handed. "That will never do," she pronounced from on high. "Don't you know that the Roman word for left is 'sinestra,' which means evil? Do you know that some societies killed babies who showed left-handedness? This just won't do, start writing with your right hand this minute!" Good grief, what a cruel, repressed bitch she was. If a teacher tried that kind of stuff today, the kid's parents would sue the school system. And win.

People may think that recycling is a relatively new thing, but it's not. Even in the 1950s, schools made money by collecting newspapers and magazines to be sold to recyclers. The school PTA sponsored these monthly or quarterly events, and there was fierce rivalry between the classes. Every teacher reminded their class every week to save their newspapers and to ask their neighbors to let them have their newspapers too. On PTA meeting night, parents would load up the car with all of their newspapers and magazines, neatly stacked and tied with twine. Slick-paper magazines brought a premium, so they were stacked separately. When you got to the school, there were signs along the driveway with the teachers' names, where you offloaded the papers. These sales of old newspapers brought the school some cash, and the winning teacher each month got recognized with big signs around the school. Kids were highly motivated to bring in the most newspapers for their class, since there was an unwritten policy that winning teachers would suspend all beatings for the remainder of the month. They could still yell at you, but during the moratorium, you didn't have to worry about corporal punishment.

The greatest joy of elementary school was, of course, recess. The word "recess" is now an anachronism, since schools now have "physical education." There's a big difference. Recess was getting to go outside and do about anything you wanted. Physical training is where everyone does what a teacher with a bullhorn tells them to do. We did have structured physical training in high school, but in elementary school, you could do most anything you wanted as long as it was legal, moral, and you didn't leave the school grounds. There were always impromptu things like softball games or basketball or marbles, but you didn't have to participate. I guess the reasoning is that today's kids will go home and spend hours inside on their cell phones or playing video games, so they need to force them to get at least a few minutes of exercise a day. Makes sense to me. And it's good for the companies that make bullhorns.

Recess wasn't the only time we got outdoors and got some exercise. We walked to school. The county only provided school buses if you lived more than a mile and a half from school. Some kids' parents drove them to school, but most kids who couldn't ride the bus walked. If it was raining, we put on our yellow raincoats and galoshes and hoofed it for miles across the unforgiving barren wilderness. Well, it seemed that way from a kid's perspective. In our case, it was actually a short stroll through suburban neighborhoods.

Lunch time at school was a mixed experience. At their appointed times, classes would march into the school's lunchroom for the daily culinary adventure. For twenty-five cents (coincidentally about the price of a can of Ken-L Ration), you got the slop du jour, consisting of a piece of rubbery mystery meat, a couple of overcooked vegetables swimming in lard, and something sweet enough to pass for dessert. And a little glass bottle of milk. There was no choice, and there were no vending machines. If you had dietary restrictions or had religious issues, you were out of luck and had to bring your lunch in a paper bag or a cute lunchbox with Roy Rogers or Mickey Mouse on it. This wasn't so bad, actually, since you at least knew what you were eating. Unfortunately, baggies hadn't been invented in the 1950s, so after your mother made your tuna fish sandwich, she wrapped it in wax paper. Canned tuna was packed in oil in those days, so by the time lunchtime rolled around, the wax paper was a sodden mess that melted into the bread, so you ended up eating lot of paper. If you carried your lunch in a lunchbox, there was a vacuum bottle inside for your milk. Unfortunately the old vacuum bottles had a paper-thin inner glass bottle that would shatter if you dropped your lunchbox or even dinged it on something hard. I went through three of the things one year, and my mom never tired of reminding me that money doesn't grow on trees.

And it was because money didn't grow on trees that my sisters and I carried our mom-made lunches to school. We weren't poor, but it would have cost a dollar a day for all four of us to buy the school lunch. And since the school lunches weren't exactly haute cuisine, that was hunky dory with us. Occasionally we did buy lunch, usually on Friday, when the main course was always fish sticks because of the Catholics, who didn't eat meat on Friday. I never figured out why fish sticks weren't meat, or why they made everyone eat fish for the three or four Catholics in our school, but it didn't matter, because I loved fish sticks (and still do).

Class field trips were the highlights of the year in elementary school. A field trip meant at least half a day out of class, which automatically made it a wonderful day. Unlike today, with the reams of paperwork and all the legal stuff, all our parents had to do was sign a short note saying it was okay for their kid to go. No ten pages of lawyer fine print about waivers and indemnification in case the bus was in an accident or your kid got ground up in a machine in a manufacturing plant. The best trip was to the local Coca Cola bottling plant. And it really was a bottling plant – in those days, you could only get Coke in those little 6½-ounce glass bottles. Atlanta is the home of the Coca Cola, and we're proud of it. Only Yankee transplants and southerners whose loyalties are suspect drink that other brand – the P-word. So it was a longstanding tradition that every kid in Atlanta made a school field trip to the local Coke bottling plant, where we marveled at the way bottles were cleaned, dried, filled, and capped, and put into heavy wooden cases all in a few minutes while zipping along an incredibly noisy production line. Then came the payoff – a free bottle of ice-cold Coke. Other field trips included the State Capitol museum, Stone Mountain for a picnic, and if the teachers really had it in for us, we got to watch the state legislature in action, assuming that enough of the legislators were out of jail on bond or had been paroled to make a quorum.

One of the rewards of being in the seventh grade was to be a safety patrolman. You got to wear a cool-looking Sam Browne belt with a badge, and you manned the crosswalks near the school. At the busiest crosswalks, you would work with an adult crossing guard who could stop traffic while kids crossed the street. At the less busy crossings, you worked with another safety patrolman ("patrolmen" being boys and girls). At these intersections, you had to roll out to the middle of the street a giant metal policeman holding his hand up. You had to roll him out twice a day, and roll him back off the road twice a day. This was fine, except that the damned things weighed a couple of hundred pounds. Making matters worse, terrorists would come by at night and push the metal policeman down a steep bank, so the next morning some poor 12-year-old schmuck had to push it back up the bank. Doctors probably wondered why so many twelve-year-olds got hernias and had to have surgery. Or maybe it was the surgeons who pushed the damned things down the hill.

But the biggest reward for a seventh grader was the annual Spring class trip to Washington, DC and New York City. For many of us, it was the longest trip we had made, and for most of us, it was our first trip to Washington or New York. And… it was a few days away from our parental units, which was the really exciting part of it. When the day finally came, we all boarded a train at the old Union Station in downtown Atlanta, and the fun was on. Most of the kids had ridden a train before, but never without their parents. After an overnight trip, we arrived at DC's Union Station, which was an awe-inspiring sight. Then we got on buses and had a day of sightseeing in the nation's capitol. We had chaperones, of course, some teachers who had volunteered, but we had a heavy numerical advantage and they were quickly overwhelmed. After doing the usual tourist spots in DC, we returned to Union Station and boarded a train for New York, where we arrived around 8:00 that night. After checking into the Hotel New Yorker, we fell instantly asleep, exhausted from a day's hiking around DC. The next morning, we got on buses and saw the highlights of New York. Having lunch at the Automat was one of the coolest things we did. The Automat was famous, and we couldn't believe we were really there ordering food in the little windows. That afternoon, we were getting short of time, so we voted to see if we would see the United Nations building or Yankee Stadium. The girls' bus voted for the UN, and the boys' bus voted for Yankee Stadium. Girls, where were their priorities? Later that night we returned on the train to Atlanta, where our parents met us at the station and took us home. End of the big adventure.

Before I close this chapter, I have to mention that all of the teachers and kids I referred to were white. From grades 1-12, there were no black kids in my schools. This was the South, and even though *Brown v. Board of Education* declared an end to "separate but equal" schools in 1954, it was more than a decade before all schools in Georgia were integrated. The City of Atlanta desegregated its schools in 1961, but it took years before other school systems in Georgia followed suit. More about growing up in the segregated South in Chapter 11.

CHAPTER 5

Arts and Entertainment

After years of war and rationing of basic commodities, Americans were more than ready to enjoy peace and prosperity. Television was the 800-pound gorilla of the entertainment industry. Americans were so enthralled with the new medium that it brought about major lifestyle changes. After making war propaganda films in the 1940s, Hollywood producers and directors began cranking out blockbusters with "casts of thousands" to lure us away from our TV sets. With professional athletes back from the war, Americans packed sports arenas again, and the World Series was televised to the delight of baseball fans.

You cannot overstate the impact of television on Americans. By the early 1950s, most US cities had three network TV stations on the air. All states had TV stations by the end of 1954. The pictures were in black and white, but by the end of the decade, color television sets were in many American homes, and more and more shows were broadcast in color. By 1954, television broadcasting revenues surpassed those of radio. Some primetime TV shows were so popular that streets were practically empty during their airing.

A barely remembered fact is that in the early 1950s, there were four TV networks: NBC, CBS, ABC, and the DuMont Television Network, each having their own local station affiliates. NBC, CBS, ABC had been radio networks for many years, so many of their affiliate radio stations added a TV side and broadcast both media. DuMont, however, had a much smaller radio network, and was never able to add enough TV stations to survive. The network folded up in 1956, but not before broadcasting a number of very successful shows like *Ted Mack's Original Amateur Hour*, *The Arthur Murray Party*, and *The Johns*

Hopkins Science Review, a Peabody Award-winning education program.

In the early days of television, stations were only on the air for parts of the day, usually signing off at 11:00 PM. The rest of the day, if you turned on the TV set, you got a "test pattern." But gradually, the on-air hours increased and TV was an all-day thing. From the start, old movies were a big hit. And I mean old movies, consisting of black and white movies from the 1930s. It wasn't until 1961, when NBC premiered its *Saturday Night at the Movies* that viewers saw movies less than fifteen or twenty years old. And the movies were in color. In Atlanta, WSB, the NBC affiliate, had a popular afternoon movie series called *Armchair Theater*. These were old pre-war movies, but the novelty of viewing *any* movie in their own home hooked viewers in this pre-VHS/DVD era.

I've seen a few of the Fifties TV shows in reruns, and for the most part, they're pretty dreadful, but there were a few shows that are still popular as reruns. Situation comedies were a huge hit with an American public ready to laugh after the grim years of depression and war. *I Love Lucy* won five Emmys, and in some US cities, the show has run continuously as reruns since production ended a half-century ago. Jackie Gleason's *The Honeymooners* also kept people home at night.

Soap operas had their beginnings in radio, but they transferred well to TV, and before long, they were a staple of daytime TV, running every weekday. With many mothers staying home to take care of their families, soap operas had a ready market of millions of women. My mom never – and I mean never – missed *Love of Life*, one of the earliest TV soap operas. *The Guiding Light* was the first TV soap (1952) and is still running today, a continuous run since the serial first aired on radio in 1937, an amazing achievement. In the 1950s, most soap operas started as 15-minute shows, but by the end of the decade, the standard length was a half-hour.

For kids, westerns were the best things on TV. Westerns had been very popular on radio, but the wide-open west came across much better on TV, even though many TV westerns were filmed on the Hollywood studio's back lots and sound stages. Three of the longest-running westerns were *Gunsmoke, The Lone Ranger*, and *Bonanza*. Westerns peaked in 1959 when there were twenty-six of them in prime time. One of the biggest new shows that year was *Rawhide*, which starred a young Clint Eastwood. Steve McQueen got his big break in *Wanted: Dead or Alive*, another popular 1950s western.

Variety shows proliferated on TV during the 1960s and 1970s, but the 1950s gave Americans a taste of how entertaining they could be. Many celebrities had their own variety shows, usually an hour in length. By far the longest running was *The Ed Sullivan Show*, airing on CBS on Sunday night at 8:00 from 1948-1971. Ed showcased every kind of act, including opera singers, rock stars, comedians, ballet dancers, and even circus acts. It was a lot like vaudeville on TV. Two of the most memorable shows were ones featuring Elvis Presley (1956) and the Beatles (1964). The Beatles were relatively unknown in the US at that time, and their performance was their American onstage debut.

Milton Berle's *Texaco Star Theater* owned Tuesday nights and was one of the most popular TV variety shows during the 1950s. Perry Como, a very popular singer, hosted his variety show, at first a 15-minute series three nights a week and later a one-hour show on Saturdays. In 1956, *The Perry Como Show* became one of the first weekly shows to be broadcast in color. Perry Como also did an annual Christmas special, one of the first TV celebrities to do so.

In 1953, *The Tonight Show* premiered on NBC, and insomniacs were in heaven, since prior to this, most TV broadcasting ended at 11:00 PM. Steve Allen was the first host, but to give him time to work on his Sunday night variety show that aired against the dominant Ed Sullivan, Ernie Kovacs hosted the show two nights a week. From 1957-1962, Jack Paar hosted the show and sometimes got in trouble with the network's censors, who were very strict about even slightly suggestive language. When Paar left the show in 1962, Johnny Carson took over and ruled the late night airwaves for the next thirty years.

Live television drama had its heyday in the 1950s. The *Hallmark Hall of Fame* productions began on NBC in 1951 and still air occasionally today. These high budget dramas brought some class to TV that was sadly lacking from most programming. Many Americans were exposed to the classical works of Shakespeare and the Broadway stage for the first time. *Playhouse 90* was a series of 90-minute dramas, a number of which were later filmed for theatrical release, including *Days of Wine and Roses* and *Requiem for a Heavyweight*. *Kraft Television Theatre* was another long-running weekly anthology for dramatic productions. *Climax!* was a mystery-suspense anthology that was very popular and is known for doing the first stage adaptation of any of Ian Fleming's James Bond novels (*Casino Royale* in 1954). There were a number of other dramatic shows, but these were some of the best known.

Game shows were an immediate hit on TV. Typically the host was a celebrity of sorts, and the contestants had to answer questions or complete tasks to advance and win. One of our favorites was *Beat the Clock*, which ran on CBS and ABC from 1950-1961. Contestants had to try to complete assigned stunts within sixty seconds while a big clock ticked down. *Truth or Consequences* (1950-1978) was a favorite quiz show where contestants had to answer a silly question. If they answered incorrectly, which was almost always the case, they had to perform an embarrassing stunt. *Concentration*, hosted by Hugh Downs, first aired in 1958 and became NBC's longest-running game show, running until 1973.

Most game shows offered small prizes and a contestant's fifteen minutes of fame. However, the Fifties saw the first TV quiz shows, and contestants had the opportunity to make big bucks on these shows. The first big quiz show was *The $64,000 Question*, followed soon afterward by a spin-off, *The $64,000 Challenge*. These shows were enormously successful, as Americans dropped everything to sweat it out with contestants as they advanced from $1 to the ultimate prize of $64,000, which was a ton of money fifty years ago. *The $64,000 Question* introduced the "isolation booth" which kept contestants from hearing answers from the audience, and in some shows, from the other contestant. *Twenty One*, the biggest money quiz show of all, premiered in 1956. *Twenty One* had a different format from other quiz shows. Two contestants in isolation booths faced each other and had to answer tough multi-part questions. It was high drama as millions of viewers watched the contestants fret and frown to come up with the answers. One very popular contestant was Charles Van Doren, a college professor, who was champion for many weeks, winning $129,000 before being toppled. Literally everyone in the country knew his name, and his picture was on the cover of *Time Magazine*. Unfortunately we learned later that some contestants were being prepped with the answers. In Van Doren's case, he was not only given the answers, the first opponent who was defeated by him was ordered to take a dive. As a result of the ensuing scandal, by the end of 1959, all of the big-money game shows were gone, and soon afterward, federal laws were passed prohibiting fixing of game shows. It was many years before big-money game shows made a comeback.

Some TV shows defied categorizing. *Queen for a Day* was one of these. It was a daytime show that ran from 1956-1964, and it was aimed at women. Kids thought it was gross and stupid, but our mothers loved it. Five days a week, the show had four wretched women who told their pathetically woeful tales ("My husband lost his job and now he needs an expensive surgery, and we have six kids and our washing machine is broken..."). The audience then clapped to indicate who was the neediest one, with an "applause meter" giving the results. Host Jack Bailey then draped a velvet robe around the teary-eyed winner and gave her some prizes to the musical accompaniment of "Pomp and Circumstance." Invariably at this point they would announce that an appliance store owner in Des Moines, Iowa, had seen the show and was giving her a new washing machine. You had to see it to believe it.

Another show that didn't fit any category was *You Asked for It*. This one was popular with the whole family, so there were no arguments about watching it. Running from 1950-1959 on ABC, it may have been TV's first reality show. Readers wrote to the show describing something they had read about or heard about, and the show recreated it, kind of like MythBusters on Discovery Channel today. The show was live, and many of the things they did were extremely dangerous. One of the most famous reenactments was William Tell shooting an apple off his son's head. On the show, they brought in a national archery champion, who shot an apple off his assistant's head. In other shows, a man wearing a bulletproof vest was shot, and in one of the most dramatic shows, an animal trainer wrestled a giant anaconda and was almost crushed to death, being saved by several assistants who pulled the snake off. The show was a huge hit for years, so much so that celebrities often showed up to chat on the air with host Art Baker.

Sports really found their place on TV. Radio still carried sports, especially baseball, the national game, but TV showed the images that radio announcers could only try to describe, and by the mid-1950s, TV was doing it in color. Millions of fans watched the Baseball Game of the Week on Saturday afternoons. The announcer was a former baseball great named Dizzy Dean, known for his butchering of the English language, with trademark phrases like "He slud into third" and "He hit that ball nine miles." At one point, enough people complained about Dizzy's misuse of the language and the example he was setting for kids that the sponsor, Falstaff Beer, announced that Dizzy would not be back the next year. Fortunately, Dizzy was so loved by baseball fans that a massive letter-writing campaign convinced Falstaff to retain him. My dad and I each wrote letters, so I'm proud to say that I had a small part in that.

The World Series was a huge hit on TV. The problem was that in the 1950s, all World Series games were played during the day. In many businesses, a lot of men (and some women) wanted to use their vacation time to stay home and watch the games. This would have caused so much absenteeism that some businesses would have had to shut down, so many businesses used a lottery system or an annual rotating system. Major League Baseball didn't figure out until 1971 that they could add a lot of viewers and thus increase advertising rates by playing World Series games at night.

Collegiate football broadcasts on TV were very popular, but NCAA rules strictly limited TV exposure in the belief that televising games would bring about a decline in attendance. In 1952, the NCAA relented and allowed one nationally televised game a week. NBC bought the broadcast rights for a then princely sum of $1,144,000. In 1955 the NCAA revised its plan, keeping eight national games while permitting regional telecasts during five specified weeks of the season. This plan was in effect until the mid-1980s, when schools and conferences were free to make their own TV deals.

Many Fifties TV shows were named for the major sponsor or were very closely associated with the sponsor. One of my favorite shows was *The Lone Ranger*, a hit western. The sponsor was Merita Bread, and kids knew they would not grow up to be like the Lone Ranger unless we ate a lot of Merita Bread. So we did. A lot of shows didn't leave it to your memory to remember who the sponsor was, so we had shows like the *DuPont Show of the Month*, *The United States Steel Hour*, and *The Alcoa Hour*, kind of like college football bowls are named today. Ironically, it was the short-lived DuMont Network that began the trend of selling advertising time to multiple sponsors, which is now a standard practice. One of the few exceptions today is the *Hallmark Hall of Fame*.

NBC made the first national broadcast in color on January 1, 1954, with the televised Tournament of Roses Parade, and sales of color TVs took off. Not! A typical color TV at that time cost about $1,200 ($10,000 in today's dollars). It wasn't until the late 1950s that color TV sets had dropped in price enough that large numbers of people could afford them. And there wasn't too much incentive to buy one, since only a few high-budget shows were broadcast in color in the 1950s. But one blockbuster show had a lot to do with increasing sales: ABC's *The Wonderful World of Disney*, which premiered in 1954, a year before Disneyland opened in California. In 1961, the show moved to NBC and the name was changed to *Walt Disney's Wonderful World of Color*. It was a marriage made in heaven. Walt Disney himself hosted the show, NBC was the network most invested in broadcasting color TV, and RCA, which made color TVs, was the major sponsor. Sales of color TVs took off. One sign of the show's influence was the Davy Crockett craze following the airing of a 1954-1955 three-part series about the Tennessee frontiersman. Just about every boy in the United States had a coonskin hat after that. It wasn't a good time for raccoons.

Television inspired many to choose their careers or hobbies. How many men and women decided to go into medicine after watching *Dr. Kildare* and *Ben Casey* in the early 1960s? How many choose to become lawyers because of *Perry Mason?* And how many youngsters grew up to be scuba divers after watching Mike Nelson on *Sea Hunt?* I can't answer the first two questions, but my wife and I are avid scuba divers today because of *Sea Hunt.*

The bottom line on TV: Americans started a head-over-heels romance with television during the 1950s that continues to this day. The Fifties are sometimes called the Golden Age of Television, because of so many innovative shows that set the trend for much of TV programming today. Never in history had a new entertainment medium captured and enthralled so many people and altered their lifestyle so much.

Television was not the only broadcast media. There was commercial radio, which had been in existence since the 1920s. Before television, radio carried the same kinds of shows as TV, including drama, comedy, westerns, mystery, sports, and even quiz shows. But radio didn't have a chance against TV. Some of the radio shows became TV shows, but many just died. In a few cases, the radio version of a show continued for a period of time after the TV version premiered. *Gunsmoke* was one of these shows. The radio and TV versions had separate casts. By the mid-1950s, most radio stations were news, weather, and music. Since most cars by this time had radios, radio had its drive-time niche, but it had a greatly reduced influence, and most advertising money migrated to TV. And radio didn't help itself with a "payola" scandal in the late 1950s when we learned that some disk jockeys were taking bribes to promote and play some songs, radio's equivalent of the TV quiz show rigging scandal.

Americans loved to go to the movies, but television hurt movie attendance enough that many theaters closed during the 1950s and early 1960s. Hollywood found innovative ways to bring audiences back. By the late 1950s, all but the lowest-budget films were in color. Movie screens got wider with Cinemascope and Cinerama. There was even a gimmicky 3-D craze for a few years. And Hollywood made blockbuster films with casts of thousands.

The Fifties was the decade for Biblical epics, including *Samson and Delilah*, *David and Bathsheba*, *The Robe*, *The Prodigal*, *The Ten Commandments*, *Solomon and Sheba*, and *Ben-Hur*. Charlton Heston rose to stardom as The *Ten Commandments* and *Ben-Hur* became two of the highest grossing films of the decade.

Westerns have always had a special place in American movies, and the 1950s westerns were better than ever, with higher production values, location shooting, and color. The decade featured classics like *Shane*, *The Searchers*, *High Noon*, *3:10 to Yuma*, and *The Big Country*. This was the golden decade for western movies, with a staggering total of more than 500 of them. Many of these were low-budget back lot pictures, but it's almost twice the number of westerns made during any other decade. That's a lot of cowboys kissing their girl and riding off into the sunset.

Science fiction was in its heyday in the Fifties. Earthlings were under constant attack from extraterrestrial aliens, and we cheered on our planet's defenders in films like *The Day the Earth Stood Still*, *The Thing from Another World*, *The War of the Worlds*, and *Forbidden Planet*. We were also under attack by monsters created by nuclear testing, and a string of low budget films like *The Beast from 20,000 Fathoms*, *Them!*, and *The Giant Gila Monster* kept kids screaming on Saturday afternoons in the movie theaters. By the mid-1950s, the Japanese were getting in on the act with low-budget horror films like *Godzilla* and *Rodan*. At last count, there have been twenty-eight Godzilla movies made, which is kind of scary when you think about it.

Alfred Hitchcock was in his prime during this period, with seven of his classic films released during the 1950s. One of his greatest hits was *Psycho*, which premiered in 1960 and is now a film classic. Amazingly, the Hollywood censors, in that pre-ratings era, did not object to the vicious stabbing scene in the shower. Instead they objected to scenes of Janet Leigh sitting on the bed in a bra and a half-slip, and to a shot of the bathroom showing the toilet, which had never been shown in a movie before. Hitchcock prevailed and the scenes were left in, but he had opened the floodgates, with hundreds of slice-and-dice horror films made in the five decades since *Psycho*.

There were plenty of serious films made during the decade. *All About Eve*, *From Here to Eternity*, *On the Waterfront*, and *Marty* won Oscars for Best Picture. *The Man in the Gray Flannel Suit* reflected societal problems in a TV-addicted nation and the estrangement of families. Parents dragged their kids to these movies, since it didn't cost much more than hiring a babysitter, but we were bored stiff with these adult films.

In the Fifties movies, Marilyn Monroe was *the* hot babe. She was huge. Both of them. What else can I say? Well, she made tight sweaters popular. And she was the cover girl on the first issue of *Playboy* magazine, published in December 1953.

Going to the movies was very different than today. In Atlanta, new films showed downtown in big, glitzy movie palaces like the Fox, Lowe's Grand, Roxy, and Paramount Theaters. Going downtown to the movies was a treat for both parents and kids. The theaters were big and ornate with dozens of nooks and crannies for kids to explore, and they had balconies where kids could throw spitballs at the people sitting below. Well, no spitballs if they were with their parents. In December 1939, one of the biggest events in Atlanta history occurred when *Gone with the Wind* premiered at the Lowe's Grand Theater. A crowd estimated at 300,000 people jammed Atlanta streets hoping to see Clark Gable, Vivien Leigh, and Olivia de Havilland, the stars of the movie. The theater burned down in the 1970s, but if it was still there, it would be hallowed ground in Atlanta.

Most of the time, however, kids went to the Saturday matinee at a neighborhood theater, where you got the "previews of coming attractions," a cartoon, and a movie, usually a "B" western or a science fiction flick. Newsreels of the week's news, which were extremely popular in the 1940s, were dropped, since TV news now served this function. Occasionally, the neighborhood theater had a "cartoon carnival," where they showed two hours of cartoons. That was a big deal, since the newer cartoons hadn't been released to TV, and seeing them in color on a big screen was a real treat.

Most movie theaters during the period only had one screen. In the 1960s, as theater owners tried to lure people from their TV sets, bigger, plusher neighborhood theaters with multiple screens started appearing. As downtown Atlanta died, the downtown theaters closed one by one, and eventually the neighborhood theaters got all the business. Families were attracted to drive-in theaters, since they were cheap, and no one had to dress up. Families often took snacks and drinks with them, and the kids could get out of the car and sit on picnic tables. Teenagers with cars especially liked drive-ins, since they could make out for a couple of hours without being yelled at by grown-ups.

Live theater was back after the war and was going strong, with some of Broadway's biggest hits coming during the decade of the 1950s. Musicals like *South Pacific, The King and I, My Fair Lady, The Music Man,* and *West Side Story* were mega-hits on Broadway that are still performed regularly today. Atlanta was about as off-off-Broadway as you could get, but we saw the movie versions of many of these hits, and we had our own summer stock tradition in Theater Under the Stars at Chastain Amphitheatre. The summer weather wasn't always cooperative, and mosquitoes could make life miserable for both the actors and the audience, but the shows were great, and Atlantans got to see a lot of celebrities. Performances went on every summer until 1968, when Theater Under the Stars moved to the new Civic

Center and became Theater of the Stars. It was the end of a long Atlanta tradition, but the Civic Center was a lot cooler and it was insect-free.

Music was as important in the Fifties as it had ever been, even more so with the introduction of portable transistor radios and phonographs. The era of the big bands and crooners was winding down in favor of rock and roll and country-western. Pianos and saxophones were replaced by guitars and drums. The origins of the term "rock and roll" are disputed, but however it started, it would be the music that defined the Fifties. Country and western music left their rural southern roots and went national. The new word in music was "Elvis." And thank God for the absence of heavy metal, grunge, rap, hip hop, and Mick Jagger (sorry, my wife made me add that last one).

Rock and roll was not a totally new kind of music. It was a mixture of blues, country music, R&B, folk music, and gospel music. Kids loved it, parents had mixed reactions, and clergymen said it was the devil's music. But it survived and thrived, thanks in part to a young Mississippian named Elvis Presley who burst onto the national scene in 1954 with a rockabilly style that teenagers went nuts over. A Texan, Buddy Holly, shared the rock and roll limelight with Presley, but his tragic death in a plane crash on February 3, 1959 will forever be known as "The Day the Music Died." Buddy, we loved you. From its early-1950s inception through the early-1960s, rock and roll music spawned new dance crazes. Sock-hops, gym dances, and home basement dance parties became the rage, and American teenagers watched Dick Clark's American Bandstand to keep up on the latest dance and fashion styles. By the early 1960s, rock and roll was gradually taking on a harder edge as music began to reflect the social and cultural changes of the times. Rock didn't die, but the simple innocence of Fifties classic rock would only occasionally be heard in the future.

During the 1950s, the nation struggled with issues of racial equality and desegregation. But music was a medium where black Americans enjoyed huge popularity and made major contributions, notably in rock and roll, R&B, jazz, and gospel music. One particular brand of rock and roll, doo-wop, is now considered to have played a key role in the success of rock and roll. Doo-wop, a style of vocal-based R&B music, developed in black communities in the 1940s and achieved mainstream popularity in the 1950s. The label doo-wop came from the "doo-wop" chant and other nonsensical syllables heard in many of the songs performed by doo-wop groups. One of the first doo-wop groups to reach national prominence was Frankie Lymon and the Teenagers ("Why Do Fools Fall in Love" and "Goody Goody"). A number of doo-wop groups were racially integrated, and eventually all-white doo-wop groups appeared.

Country and western music grew in popularity during the 1950s as city dwellers took to the music. Also, country and western music was no longer only a southern phenomenon. People all over the nation were listening to the music. Many urban radio stations went to an all country-western music format during the 1950s and 1960s. Fans listened to the *Grand Ole Opry* and the *Louisiana Hayride* on radio, and in 1955, ABC-TV began broadcasting the *Ozark Jubilee*, "live from the heart of the Ozarks" (Springfield, Missouri).

Reading was still a favorite pastime for both adults and kids, although TV, radio, and phonographs cut into reading time. Glossy magazines like *Saturday Evening Post*, *Life*, and *Look* were immensely popular, and millions of Americans subscribed to them. The popularity of TV led to the birth of a new magazine in 1953: *TV Guide*. Libraries were used extensively, and almost all families had a library card. Book clubs flourished as Americans tried to keep up with the latest novels. *Reader's Digest*, a monthly magazine, and *Reader's Digest Condensed Books* were anthologies of recent articles and books for people who wanted a quick read.

Most of the big widely-circulated weekly or bi-weekly magazines are gone now, but fifty years ago people looked forward to the day they were delivered by the postman. *Saturday Evening Post*, *Life*, and *Look* were the big three, and each was different. *Saturday Evening Post*, first published in the nineteenth century, was famous for its cover art by Norman Rockwell and its short stories and articles. Rockwell was famous for his paintings of life in an idyllic America that many people longed for. *Life* was a photojournalism magazine whose motto was "To see Life; see the world." Some of the most dramatic stories of the twentieth century were documented in *Life*, including Robert Capa's photography of the D-Day landings in Normandy. *Look* was a bi-weekly magazine that emphasized photography with less emphasis on articles.

Another magazine that has to be mentioned was *Mad Magazine*, first published in 1952. It was an almost instant success. *Mad* was pure satire, skewering every aspect of American life and culture, and we laughed ourselves silly. Not everyone laughed, however. *Mad* was sued a number of times, winning some cases and losing some. Since the magazine had no paid advertising, they were free to lampoon anyone and anything, and they did so with a vengeance. Alfred E. Neuman, *Mad*'s goofy-looking "What, me worry?" kid, was an icon by the end of the decade.

As popular as magazines were, comic books were more important to kids. Most comic books in this era were basically expanded versions of the newspaper comic strips. Comic books sold for ten cents, and kids traded them like baseball cards. Like most entertainment media, comic book sales declined once TV entered, but kids loved them, and parents didn't object, since comic books helped us learn to read, and we didn't make much noise while reading them. Many comic books were about cartoon characters like Donald Duck, Casper the Friendly Ghost, and Archie Comics (the antics of a group of zany teenagers). Older kids loved superhero action comic books about Superman, Batman, and Wonder Woman.

Books, of course, were important to both adults and kids, and after the paper shortages during WWII, publishers were happy to be printing again. Since books were expensive and mass market paperbacks were not available for many titles, the school and local libraries saw a lot of use. Book-of-the-Month Club had many subscribers who wanted to keep up with the latest bestsellers without spending too much money. It was a good alternative to the library, where bestsellers were hard to find, with so many people checking them out.

American literature had a banner decade in the 1950s, and many of the decade's books are now classics. For teenagers, the book of the decade was J.D. Salinger's *The Catcher in the Rye* (1951), an instant classic that still sells a quarter of a million copies a year. Counterculture and the "Beat Generation" had successes in railing against materialism and conformity with Allen Ginsberg's poetry and Jack Kerouac's novel *On the Road* (1957), another novel that still sells a lot of copies. William Goldman, a British author, had a huge hit with *Lord of the Flies*, a 1954 novel about school boys stranded on an island. By the end of the decade, the book was required reading in many high schools and colleges.

It was a great decade for fantasy, with J.R.R. Tolkien's epic *Lord of the Rings* trilogy in 1954-1955 and *The Lion, the Witch, and the Wardrobe* by C.S. Lewis. Science fiction peaked in the 1950s with some of the finest works by Ray Bradbury (*The Martian Chronicles, Fahrenheit 451*), Robert A. Heinlein (*Tunnel in the Sky*), and Isaac Asimov (*I, Robot*).

A number of novels published during the decade had profound influence on American culture and thought. Ayn Rand's *Atlas Shrugged* (1957) was a critically acclaimed novel focusing on the evils of socialism. *Peyton Place* (1956) by Grace Metalious was a blockbuster about the sordid secrets of a small New England town. It was on the New York Times bestseller list for more than a year. *Lolita* (1955) was an international bestseller and one of the most controversial books of the twentieth century with its story of an older man's infatuation with a 12-year-old girl. Leon Uris' *Exodus* (1958) novel thrilled us with a story told against the backdrop of the founding of the State of Israel. It was the biggest bestseller in the US since *Gone with the Wind* was published in 1936.

Ian Fleming, the creator of Agent 007, published seven of his twelve James Bond novels during the 1950s. They weren't profound and they had little influence on society, but millions of readers passed a lot of enjoyable hours reading about 007's exploits against the arch villains of SMERSH and SPECTRE. All of the James Bond novels were eventually made into movies, but in the 1950s, we had only the literary version of 007.

It was one of my mother's fondest wishes that she would pass on to me her own love of reading. When I was just a kid in the mid-1950s, she came home one day with a stack of children's classics: *Black Beauty*, *Treasure Island*, *Adventures of Huckleberry Finn*, plus some contemporary novels that she thought I would like. This was the start of a lifelong love of reading for me. It makes up for throwing my old baseball cards away. Well, almost.

With all the players back from the war, collegiate and professional sports were once again a major entertainment media. Baseball was the national game in professional sports, and football was second. In Atlanta, we filled Ponce de Leon Park to watch our beloved minor league baseball team, the Atlanta Crackers, play the Memphis Chicks, Birmingham Barons, and other teams in the Southern Association. And we dreamed of having a major league team, which we finally got in 1966 when the Braves moved from Milwaukee to Atlanta. The other big team in town was the Georgia Tech Yellow Jackets, who rewarded us with a national championship in football in 1952. That wouldn't happen again for almost forty years.

The National Football League and the National Basketball Association had plenty of fans, but in Atlanta, hundreds of miles from any franchise city, we didn't care that much. In 1960 the American Football League was created, and the competition between the two leagues for the top college players was fierce, sparking increased interest in the sport. In Atlanta, we longed for our own team. In the early 1960s, a temporary stadium called America Field was built in an Atlanta suburb for a series of American Football League exhibition games. Partly as a result of this pressure, the National Football League awarded an expansion franchise to Atlanta in 1965, and in 1966 the Atlanta Falcons began play. In 1968, the St. Louis Hawks of the National Basketball Association moved to Atlanta, so finally we had major league teams for the big three sports. Unfortunately, for most of the years they've been here, the Falcons and Hawks have sucked. At least the Braves have given us a World Series champion.

In the South, stock car racing was growing rapidly in popularity, and in 1959, NASCAR's first Daytona 500 was run. In the 1950s, the race cars really were stock cars off the production line, with only a few modifications for safety and performance. It's a different sport today, with the huge super speedways, network TV contracts, and cars that are built from the ground up for racing.

CHAPTER 6

Politics and Culture

I was tempted to include a separate chapter on politics during the 1950s decade. But I'm telling this from the viewpoint of a kid growing up during that period, and what does a kid know or care about politics? So I named the chapter "Politics and Culture." When you get right down to it, the politics and culture of a people are so intertwined that it's difficult to separate them. Certainly our form of government affects our culture as well as our politics. Fortunately the United States is a republic with a constitution safeguarding the rights of the individual and the minority, not a democracy as many people believe. Under our constitution, we have rule by law, so our politicians can't just change the rules on a whim, although it seems that way sometimes. This has contributed enormously to our stability and growth.

If there is a single word that describes the 1950s, I would suggest the word "dynamic." Enormous changes took place in American society during the decade. The United States and the Soviet Union emerged from World War II as the world's superpowers, and the Cold War was on, with its ever present threat of nuclear annihilation. Even with increasingly large military budgets, Americans found that we could have both "guns *and* butter" in the quest for wealth and a better lifestyle than their Depression-era parents had. Capitalism reigned supreme as we competed against the Communists and their government-controlled economy.

Dwight D. Eisenhower was elected President in 1952, taking over from the feisty Harry Truman. It was the first time a Republican President had occupied the White House since Herbert Hoover departed in 1933 for the incoming Franklin D. Roosevelt. There were no cheers from the South, however. Most Southern states had voted for Eisenhower's Democrat opponents in both the 1952 and 1956 elections, which Eisenhower won by a landslide. In Georgia, it would have been more socially acceptable to have a venereal disease than to have it known you voted Republican, such was the hatred of Republicans that persisted for almost a century after the Civil War and Reconstruction. To this day, my mother, who is not a liberal, has never voted for a Republican for any office. Times did change, and eventually the South turned away from the Democrats, but in the 1950s, the Democrats had solid control of the region.

But Eisenhower, who had led the Allies to victory in Europe, was the right man for the job, regardless of his party affiliation. The nation's economy had been heavily controlled by the federal government for the previous two decades of depression and war. Eisenhower simply got out of the way and let the free enterprise system work, and the nation grew and prospered. Standards of living rose throughout the decade as Americans drove their new cars, enjoyed the marvelous new medium of television, and explored ways to enjoy their leisure time.

From my view as a kid, politics was mostly fun. Candidates for state and local office often held big rallies where, after listening to long-winded speeches, you got free barbecue or fried fish with all the trimmings. These rallies were held in public parks with lots of playground equipment for kids, so many families made a day of it, and the kids had a great time.

What wasn't so fun for kids was that presidential nominating conventions were shown on TV on all three networks, replacing our favorite shows. To kids, these things were about as exciting as watching grass grow. But our parents loved them. For the first time, they could watch the conventions live and see as well as hear politicians wheeling and dealing to nominate a candidate. There was a lot of human drama in the conventions then. Conventions weren't the dull scripted pep rallies that they are now. Unlike today, candidates seldom went into a convention with the nomination already in their pocket, so conventions were knockdown rhetorical brawls and deal-making to see who was the last one standing, so for grownups at least, it made for great

TV. With today's state primary system, one candidate often locks up his party's nomination months before the convention. Now that I'm grown up, I'd love to see nominating conventions like they were in the old days, but it ain't likely to happen.

The 1960 Presidential election was one of the most memorable elections of the 20th century, pitting the Democrat nominee John F. Kennedy against the Republican Richard Nixon. It was one of the closest races in our history, with Kennedy winning the popular vote by less than a 0.1% margin. It was the first election where the two candidates debated on television. It was the first national election where the two newest states, Alaska and Hawaii, participated. And Kennedy was the first Roman Catholic to be elected President. It's difficult today to understand why Kennedy's religion was such an issue, but it was. The majority of Americans were Protestants, and many of them believed that a Catholic President would take orders from the Pope in Rome. Balancing this, however, was Kennedy's support of Martin Luther King Jr., which earned him many black votes.

Until 1963, Georgia was unique in its voting system for governor. Under the County Unit System, which worked something like the Electoral College in Presidential elections, counties had a certain number of electoral votes depending on their population: the largest counties got three votes, the middle tier of counties got two votes, and the smallest counties got one vote. So the three smallest counties, with a total population of perhaps 5,000 people, could equal the vote of Fulton County, which had half a million people. Since the small rural counties, with only one-third of the state population, had almost sixty percent of the votes, most gubernatorial candidates were from rural areas. It also meant that they didn't need to campaign in the cities, and that's why it mattered to city kids: no free barbecues or fish fries from gubernatorial candidates.

Until the mid-1950s, most American homes were very small, often with only two bedrooms and one bathroom. Our family lived in one of these cracker boxes. By the middle of the decade, homebuilders were putting up houses at a record pace as returning soldiers wanted a big house and a yard for their new families. So many new houses were built during the decade that by 1960, an estimated 25% of all housing in the US had been built in the 1950s. The standard new home in Atlanta had three bedrooms, 1½ or two bathrooms, a "picture window," and a carport. The house usually had real hardwood floors instead of plywood and cheap carpeting. And they featured the luxury of central heating and air conditioning. In Atlanta in the mid-1950s, a typical new house sold for about $20,000, which with a minimum down payment, left you with about a $100 per month mortgage. A lot of homes during this period were purchased with Veteran's Administration (VA) mortgages at very low interest rates.

Newspapers played a huge role in reporting the news and current events. In the 1940s, circulation began to drop due to radio, and with the advent of TV, circulation numbers began a steady decline that continues even today. Nevertheless, in the 1950s, most adults read the newspaper for news and features. Kids read the comic strips and sports. Many cities had more than one daily newspaper, and competition to attract readers was often fierce, with price wars, promotions and contests, and new features like crossword puzzles and word games. TV news shows were still finding their way, so newspapers played the major role of investigative journalism, especially for ferreting out wrongdoing at the local level.

Newspaper editorials had enormous influence on public opinion. Editorial cartoons also shaped opinions and were often controversial. "Letters to the Editor" sections let readers share their ideas and opinions. Before online blogs and forums developed in the 1990s, newspapers were the most widely read and most effective forums for public debate. Unlike today, when editorial letters can be emailed and published as soon as the next day, in the pre-Internet era, letters had to be mailed in, and by the time they were published, the topic may not have been as timely.

Newspapers came to the forefront in the Fifties during the struggle for civil rights. In the South, many newspaper publishers and editors were adamantly for segregation of races, and this had a major influence on their readers. In Atlanta, home of Martin Luther King Jr., The Atlanta Constitution and Atlanta Journal's editors strongly supported the civil rights movement, as did Atlanta mayor William B. Hartsfield, and this had much to do with Atlanta's relatively peaceful desegregation of public schools and parks.

By the mid-1950s, both national network and local TV station news programs were becoming increasingly sophisticated and influential, and many people turned to news broadcasts for their daily news. Edward R. Murrow, now a TV legend, is usually considered the pioneer of network TV news with his weekly CBS show *See it Now*. The network nightly news shows began as brief 15-minute summaries of the day's national and international highlights, but had expanded to thirty minutes by the early 1960s. NBC's *Huntley-Brinkley Report* with Chet Huntley and David Brinkley was the most watched news show, but other well-known newscasters included CBS's Douglas Edwards and Walter Cronkite, and ABC's John Charles Daly. It's hard to believe today, with the daily hour-long network news shows and numerous news features throughout the week that the network news shows were only fifteen minutes, but in those days, TV executives looked at news shows more as a public service than as a revenue source.

Television news in the Fifties was a far cry from news shows today. TV news in the 1950s was very simple and straightforward. Until 1956, when videotape came into use, newsworthy events were filmed, with the film being sent to a TV network station that could develop and edit it, then transmit it by microwave to the network. As a practical matter, film of most news events was often not shown on TV until the following day.

With very few exceptions, network TV newscasts were anchored by white males. Some local TV news shows did feature white women, but in the 1950s, there were almost no black men or women on-camera. This would change in the 1960s, when TV newscasts gradually became more inclusive of women and blacks, but TV news in the 1950s was the dominion of white males.

After watching the network and local news, most Americans stayed glued to their TV sets, with network programming beginning at 7:00 PM instead of 8:00 as it is now. TV was a hot new medium that quickly relegated radio to the back seat. You had to be living then to know just how influential TV was in the average American's life. On Tuesday nights, the entire country came to a virtual standstill during the hour that Milton Berle was on NBC. The whole country tuned in to see what outrageous costume "Uncle Miltie" would open the show with. Some movie theaters and restaurants closed early on Tuesdays, unable to compete with the success of the show. Sales of TV sets soared after his show premiered. It's no wonder that Berle was called "Mr. Television." Many highly successful TV shows followed, but Milton Berle had the show that got Americans hooked on TV and made couch potatoes of us.

As outrageous as Milton Berle was, the rest of us were pretty mundane by comparison. The Fifties decade was largely a time of social and political conservatism. Men's hair was short, and women's hemlines were below the knee. Most women wore one-piece bathing suits, although two-piece suits weren't frowned on if they didn't show too much skin. In TV shows about married couples, like *I Love Lucy* and *I Married Joan*, the couples wore pajamas at night and always had separate beds. The word "pregnant" was verboten on TV. Women were either "having a baby" or were "with child." With nothing more intimate than a quick peck on the cheeks, there appeared to be a wave of immaculate conceptions in those days by married people on TV. And these couples *were* married. Cohabitation by unmarried men and women was far too licentious for TV in that era.

It would be impossible to write about 1950s culture without at least a passing mention of pop art. Pop art developed in the United States in the late 1950s as a reaction to the elitist art culture of the era. Put simply: lighten up, folks, art can be fun. Pop art took its inspiration from popular mass culture, including advertising, comic books, television, and other ordinary cultural objects. The best known pop artist in the US was Andy Warhol.

71

Warhol's most famous works were in the 1960s, but he was a leader in the new art form by the mid-1950s with his fanciful drawings for advertisements. During the 1960s, Warhol became a cultural icon with his paintings of American products like Campbell's Soup cans and paintings of celebrities such as Marilyn Monroe. A very talented person with words as well as a paintbrush, Warhol coined the phrase "15 minutes of fame," which alone would have been enough to cement his place in history.

The 1920s had its "Lost Generation," and the 1950s had its counterpart in the "Beat Generation." As pop artists rejected traditional art, the Beat Generation writers rejected mainstream American values, particularly materialism. Often called beatniks, besides their avant-garde writing, they often experimented with drugs and explored the limits of their sexuality, both of which shocked conservative Americans. The stereotypical beatnik was Maynard G. Krebs from the TV show *The Many Loves of Dobie Gillis*, but Krebs was just a comic character who played bongo drums, went into spasms if the word "work" was mentioned, and served as a foil to the conservative, straitlaced Dobie Gillis. The real beatniks such as writers Allen Ginsberg and Jack Kerouac weren't much like Krebs. Their writing was heavily into drugs, sex, and potty language, and resulted in liberalizing what could be published in the United States. During the social and political upheavals of the 1960s, beatniks more or less morphed into "hippies," but the Beat Generation played a significant role in setting the stage for the counterculture of the Sixties.

The beatnik culture had minimal impact on conservative Americans, but such was not the case when Alfred Kinsey, a biologist, published two reports, *Sexual Behavior in the Human Male* in 1948, followed in 1953 by *Sexual Behavior in the Human Female*. Both books hit the top of bestseller lists and made Kinsey an instant celebrity. The reports were extremely controversial, especially when Kinsey later acknowledged that he had interviewed a number of pedophiles about their experiences with children and had not reported their names to authorities. With Kinsey's stated belief that delayed sexual experience was psychologically harmful to an individual, he laid the groundwork for the sexual revolution of the Sixties.

Every decade contributes its own slang words and expressions to the language, and the Fifties were no exception. The slang wasn't as colorful as the Sixties, with its drug and protest culture, but we had a few good ones that took hold and are still used today. "Cool" was undoubtedly our number one contribution to the English language. We used it as an adjective, as in "She's pretty cool," and as a verb like "Cool it." A troublemaker was "cruisin' for a bruisin'," and no one wanted to be around a "party pooper" or a "nerd." "Holy cow" was a favorite expression if you weren't Hindu. Beatniks contributed a lot of slang, including "hip" (someone who is in the know), "drag" (a bore), "Daddy-O" (just about anyone), and "square" (normal people). Hot-rodders added their own lingo that became part of the language with words like "blow off" (to beat in a race), "cream" (to badly damage a car), and "souped up." If someone said "See ya later, alligator," the required response was "After while, crocodile."

Patriotism was in during the Fifties, and men served two years or more in the armed forces, many of them being drafted. Few men wanted to be drafted, but it was considered to be an obligation to be fulfilled. A young man's rite of passage included registering with the local draft board on his eighteenth birthday. Many high schools had Reserve Officers' Training Corps (ROTC) programs, and virtually all male college students were required to take two years of ROTC (this federal requirement for land-grant colleges and universities was dropped in 1965).

The 1950s was a time when individualism and self-reliance were considered admirable qualities, and socialism was a four-letter word. The Vietnam War and social movements in the 1960s and 1970s would rip all that apart, but in the 1950s, most Americans felt secure in their belief in God and country. Church attendance was very high during the decade, and Christmas was Christmas, not the "holiday season." Schools started the day with the Pledge of Allegiance and the Lord's Prayer. In 1954, the words "under God" were added to the Pledge of Allegiance. Few people objected to school prayer until 1960 when Madelyn Murray O'Hair, an atheist, filed a lawsuit in her local school district in which she asserted that it was unconstitutional for her son to be compelled to participate in Bible readings and prayer. Eventually the Supreme Court ruled in her favor.

The Fifties were remarkably free of the extremist religious cult suicides and murders that made headline news in later decades, such as the Peoples Temple massacre in Guyana in 1978, the Branch Davidian deaths in 1993, and the Heaven's Gate mass suicide in California in 1997. The Fifties did, however, see the founding of the Church of Scientology. Created in 1953 by science fiction writer L. Ron Hubbard, the "church" taught some mumbo-jumbo about reincarnation and ancient space travelers. Unfortunately for members, these fantastic secrets were only revealed after they turned over all their assets to Hubbard. For reasons that escape me, Scientology still exists, and suckers continue to turn over their money to the charlatans who run it.

Styles and fashion had their own distinctive look in the Fifties. Blue jeans went from being outdoor work clothes to being popular leisure wear, and the formality of earlier decades gave way to a more casual look as men saw movie stars like James Dean wearing jeans. Casual wear did not, however, extend to the workplace. Men who worked in offices were expected to wear suits or jackets with ties, and the well dressed man always wore a hat while outside. In those days before wash and wear, the businessman's white dress shirts were always starched and pressed (and uncomfortable as hell with the stiff, starched neck).

Most women wore dresses or blouses and skirts. Women could wear pants, but many workplaces and schools didn't allow them. One new style of women's clothing came into prominence in the Fifties: the maternity dress. With the millions of Baby Boomers being born during the decade, fashion designers turned their efforts toward stylish maternity wear. Maternity dresses were usually in two pieces with loose tops and stretchy skirts. They were almost like uniforms – you could spot a pregnant woman a mile away.

It seemed like every woman's ultimate fashion goal was to own a mink coat. In those idyllic days before PETA moonbats were running around loose, there was little stigma to having a fur coat, and a mink coat didn't mean just keeping up with the Joneses, it meant getting ahead of them, which was the name of the game then. It didn't matter that it seldom got cold enough in Atlanta to wear a mink coat, women still paraded them around at social functions, even during the steaming hot summers.

With all the Baby Boomer kids, clothing manufacturers were cranking out new products as fast as they could get them to stores. Kids' clothes were more upscale and less frumpy than in previous decades, but they weren't nearly as skimpy or suggestive as they are now. Teenagers, of course, had a rebellious streak fueled by some of their rock and roll and movie heroes, and many young people dressed with more individuality than Americans were used to seeing. Tight pants, black leather jackets, and longer hair were for teenage boys who wanted the punk look. Teenage girls expressed themselves with tight skirts and elaborate hairdos. But most kids just wore their department store clothes and stared at their avant-garde classmates with a mixture of disdain and wannabe envy.

People stayed in touch with out-of-town friends and relatives by letter writing. Today, letter writing with pen and ink seems so archaic, but that's the way it was then. Long distance telephone calling was expensive, and you couldn't transmit pictures of new babies or your new car over the telephone, so people wrote to each other. The postage for a one-ounce letter was only three cents at the beginning of the decade and four cents at the end, so anyone could afford to write. The actual writing was done with a pencil or a refillable ink pen at the beginning of the decade, but by the mid-1950s, the new Papermate and Bic ballpoint pens were selling in the hundreds of millions. Letter writing was an art, and most people cared about their penmanship, spelling, grammar, and punctuation. Unlike emails, which are practically instantaneous, letters did take time to arrive. First class mail was carried by trucks and trains, and if you wanted air mail, it cost substantially more, so most mail traveled by ground and could take several days to go from one coast to the other. If you needed to send a message faster than the postal service could deliver it, a Western Union telegraph was an option, but unfortunately, their famous Candygram was not available until the 1960s.

If Americans didn't want to write their relatives, they could visit them, even if they lived hundreds of miles away. Americans have always had itchy feet, and personal mobility has always ranked high on our list of needs, whether it was a horse, a bicycle, or a car. In the Fifties, there were a lot of transportation options, including the railroads, which had served travelers since the early 19th century, and intercity bus service, which dated from the early 20th century. For the first time, however, most Americans had their own motorized vehicles which could go anywhere and weren't bound by a schedule, and there were roads and infrastructure to support the demand for travel. Americans made the most of their newfound freedom to travel anywhere, and this was reflected in our car-crazy culture of the 1950s.

Sickness and disease were as troublesome as they are today, perhaps more so. Contagious diseases like smallpox, whooping cough, and diphtheria still existed, but vaccinations had reduced them to a very low incidence. Polio reached epidemic levels by the mid-1950s and scared the daylights out of parents, but vaccines were developed that stopped the disease in its tracks. But we didn't worry about AIDS, genital herpes, or avian flu. We also were the first generation of Americans to be treated with antibiotics from the day we were born.

Doctors didn't have most of the marvelous tests available today, such as MRIs and CT scans. With nothing much more advanced than X-Rays, many patients heard the dreaded words "exploratory surgery," which meant that a surgeon cut on you and poked around until he found the problem. Many times, especially if they found cancer, they just sewed you back up, and you went home to die. Returning military doctors learned about trauma the hard way in the war, so if you had a gunshot wound, someone in the nearest emergency room would know what to do.

Many surgeries and treatments that are done routinely today on an outpatient basis or require only a brief hospital stay were a big deal fifty years ago. Even a simple hernia or hemorrhoids required a few days in the hospital. Laparoscopic procedures were many years in the future, so surgeons cut you up like a filet and sewed you back together afterward. For a gallbladder removal, instead of a quick in-and-out through your belly button and back to work in a few days, they made a huge incision and lifted out your gallbladder. It hurt for a long time afterward. I know, I've been there and have the big scar to prove it. All types of surgery were like that. In 1966, my mother was in the hospital for almost a week for a cataract removal. Today she would be in and out of an eye clinic in a couple of hours. I'm not criticizing doctors, I'm just pointing out how far medical technology has come in the last half-century. It's mind-boggling to think where we'll be fifty years from now. Maybe surgeons will operate from the fourth dimension where they can repair or remove organs without even breaking the skin.

No one ever accused Americans of being overly cultured, and in the 1950s, we outdid ourselves for tackiness, from our flashy cars with whitewall tires to vinyl slipcovers on our furniture. Europeans ridiculed us as being a cultural backwater, despite our having saved their asses from the Germans for the second time in the 20th century, but earning little gratitude for it. We couldn't have cared less what they thought. Anyway, how can they say we weren't cultured – an American created Muzak!

The Fifties were probably the last decade when Americans didn't worry much about crime, and many people didn't even lock their doors except at night. The early 1960s brought a wave of violent crime that changed attitudes from complacency to fear almost overnight. Kitty Genovese, a young working woman, was stabbed to death in Queens, New York in 1964 while many of her neighbors watched or heard her screams and did nothing. 1966 brought two mass murders that still resonate with their violent, wanton killings. In July, a ne'er-do-well named Richard Speck methodically killed eight young nurses in a Chicago apartment. Only two weeks later, Charles Whitman murdered fourteen people in Austin, Texas, most of them on the University of Texas campus. Feelings of safety, even in one's home, vanished as people locked their doors and armed themselves. But in the 1950s, people still felt safe in their homes and neighborhoods. And if an intruder broke into your house, you could always crack them over the head with your kid's bronzed shoes.

CHAPTER 7

Shopping

Shopping in the United States changed dramatically in the 1950s. It was an era when small mom 'n' pop grocery stores gave way to big supermarket chain stores. For the first time, Americans could get all their groceries in one large self-service store instead of going to separate butcher shops, bakeries, dairies, and produce stores. There were several large supermarket chains, with the leaders being A&P, Piggly Wiggly, and Kroger. The major supermarket chains in the South were Winn-Dixie and Colonial Stores, which was later renamed Big Star. Competition was fierce as these chains expanded and grew. One very successful marketing tool was the issuing of trading stamps. The biggest names were S&H Green Stamps and Gold Bond Stamps. You got stamps when you made a purchase, with the amount of stamps depending on the amount of the purchase. Each stamp brand had catalogs with merchandise you could get with the filled stamp books at the stamp company's store or by mail order. The stamps helped to ensure customer loyalty to a particular supermarket chain by encouraging the customer to shop at that chain to get enough books filled to get merchandise. When supermarkets advertised double stamp days, it was bedlam in the aisles as people filled their carts to get extra stamps.

Going through the checkout line in a supermarket could be a grueling experience. As with all stores during the Fifties, there were no lasers and barcodes to scan. Everything had a price marked on it, and the cashier rang up each item separately on a cash register, a very time-consuming process. Since this was prone to errors, most people stood there while they checked their receipt, especially to make sure that sale items were rung up correctly. By the time you got through the line, you knew the life history of at least a couple of people in line with you.

Banks were the same way. 1950s banks had a lot more tellers than they do today. There was no direct deposit, no ATMs, and no electronic banking. If you needed to get money or make a deposit, you went to the bank. Bank buildings were a lot bigger then, since they had a lot more teller windows, and there were only a few suburban branches.

There were promotions similar to trading stamps that were advertised on radio stations. One of these was "Bid-a-Bucks," where you got fake money when you bought stuff at certain merchants. In Atlanta, every few months they had a Bid-a-Bucks Night at Ponce de Leon Park, where our minor league baseball team, the Crackers, played. They had a lot of good stuff to bid on, but people got frustrated and unhappy pretty quickly when they got badly outbid by people who had pooled their bucks with other people. After the first couple of Bid-a-Buck Nights, it turned into a bidding war between churches and schools and civic organizations, and it got ugly sometimes when a school PTA outbid a church and everyone started yelling at each other. So Bid-a-Bucks died a quick death, one of those ideas that sounded better on paper than it turned out to be.

Except for restaurants, movie theaters, and pharmacies, most stores were closed on Sunday. Many states had religious-based "Blue Laws" that enforced these closings. Most Blue Laws have since been repealed or declared unconstitutional, but in the 1950s, you didn't do any shopping on Sunday. On weekdays, most stores closed by 6:00 or 7:00, so a working person usually shopped for groceries on the way home from work. These early closings weren't required by law, they were just tradition. In Georgia, alcohol sales are still prohibited on Sunday, although some local governments allow restaurants to sell alcohol by the drink.

The 1950s saw the development of the first big shopping malls, but the modern enclosed, climate-controlled suburban malls anchored by major department stores didn't really get going until the 1960s. The 1950s malls were just glorified strip malls, sometimes running for several hundred feet along a busy road or occupying a major street corner. The stores were separated from the street by huge paved parking lots with acres of parking. The biggest mall in our neighborhood was anchored by a supermarket, but by the end of the 1950s, most major suburban malls included one or more department stores.

The suburbs had plenty of drugstores, supermarkets, hardware stores, and service stations, but for serious shopping, you went downtown. Department stores were the big attraction, since they sold almost everything. In Atlanta, the main department stores were Rich's, Davison's, and Sears. For kids, it was a real treat to ride downtown with their mothers on a trolley and explore these huge stores. You could have a lot of fun just "window shopping," ogling the elaborate displays in the store windows. One reason I loved Rich's was that it was one of the few places we went that had elevators and escalators. Elevators were a real hoot to ride. Automatic elevators weren't in wide service until well into the Sixties, so there were still elevator operators in their spiffy uniforms calling out the floors and which departments were on each floor.

Rich's was an Atlanta tradition, and it was a special place for Atlantans. You could buy almost anything there, and there was a bargain basement where you could get decent clothes on sale dirt cheap. The Magnolia Tea Room was Rich's in-store restaurant, and it was one of the best restaurants in town. Rich's was a magical place for kids at Christmas time, with the lighting of the Great Tree on Thanksgiving night, and the trips to see Santa and ride the Pink Pig monorail through the toy department. The store had the most liberal return policy of any of the department stores. You could bring anything back for a refund with no questions asked. There were stories about brides buying expensive wedding dresses and bringing them back for a refund *after* the wedding. It was that kind of place, a beloved Atlanta tradition. Sadly, the downtown Rich's store that had brought so much joy to Atlanta kids closed in 1991, and the building was torn down to be replaced by a federal office building. Some of the suburban Rich's stores built when Rich's expanded in the 1960s still exist, but they're under the Macy's name now. And I don't think they give refunds on wedding dresses.

Clothing was *not* optional in the Fifties. Americans were long past the Victorian era, but the Great Depression years had seen a toning down of fashions, and colors tended to be muted. Americans were ready to look good again. Synthetic fibers like nylon were being produced, but natural fibers like cotton still predominated. Mercifully, spandex wasn't invented until 1959. Many clothes were homemade, and most women had a Singer sewing machine that they knew how to use. I remember my mother buying paper patterns and fabric at cloth stores, pinning the patterns to the fabric, cutting out the pieces with a pair of pinking shears, then sewing them together. Mothers made clothes mostly for themselves and their daughters.

The big home improvement chains like Home Depot and Lowe's didn't exist in the Fifties, so the neighborhood hardware store was where you went for home repairs or improvements. They also sold just about anything else you wanted. There were some hardware chains like Ace, True Value, and Economy Auto, but there were a lot of independent hardware stores too. Either way, they were homey places where you got to know the proprietors and the people who worked there. You could buy almost anything there: guns and ammunition, car repair parts, tools, nuts and bolts, lumber, paint, rope, electrical parts, light bulbs, flower and vegetable seeds, animal feed, whatever. They had it, and the people who worked there could tell you how to use it. In a really good hardware store, you couldn't leave without buying *something*.

In the pre-Internet era, mail order was huge, especially in rural areas where the nearest department store could be many miles away over dirt roads. Big department store chains like Sears & Roebuck, Montgomery Ward, and J.C. Penney printed and mailed huge catalogs every summer and winter, plus a special catalog for Christmas. In the suburbs, where there were big department stores near at hand, we didn't do much mail order with these stores, but it was always a big day when the postman delivered the new catalog (and they probably got hernias from carrying them, since they weighed several pounds). The big mail order chains each tried to outdo each other, and their catalogs were marvels with their slick-paper printing and even some use of color. The Sears annual Christmas catalog was known as the "Wish Book" because of all the toys in it. My sister Janis and I fought over who got to peruse it first. For many boys the catalogs, with their underwear and bra advertisements using real models, gave the first peek at half-naked women. Some pretty racy stuff for that era, but growing up in a small house with four females, I had already seen it all. Well, most of it.

Even though we had department stores nearby, we did use mail order for a lot of things. There were always tempting advertisements for toys, gadgets, or other goodies in newspapers and magazines, as well as in TV commercials. You sent in your money and waited "four to six weeks" (that's what every ad said) for delivery. Delivery was always by the postman, since UPS and FedEx didn't exist then. The toys and gadgets never worked like the ads or commercials claimed, but we were suckers, so we kept ordering the stuff and waiting anxiously for the postman to come.

I said we were suckers. That's not strictly true, but advertisers knew how to pull our strings. Advertising in the Fifties had evolved light-years from the crude advertising of earlier decades, and now advertisers had a new medium – television – that forced viewers to watch their commercials. Millions of dollars were being spent on consumer motivational research, which is a fancy term for determining how to get customers to buy product A instead of product B, C, or D. *The Hidden Persuaders*, a classic book by Vance Packard that was published in 1957, detailed the psychology and subliminal tactics used by advertisers. Whatever they were doing, it was working. We were buying cars, TV sets, toys, electronics, food, candy, cigarettes, beer, soft drinks, soap, toothpaste, and other consumer products in quantities that would have been unbelievable to the previous generation.

American companies were quick to jump into TV advertising, and inspired ad agencies created some of the most famous commercials in those early years of TV. Everyone knew that Kentucky Fried Chicken was "finger lickin' good," but if you got heartburn from it, relief was just a "plop, plop, fizz, fizz" away with Alka-Seltzer. We also knew that our Timex wristwatch could "take a licking and keep on ticking," and Pepsodent toothpaste hooked us with "You'll wonder where the yellow went when you brush your teeth with Pepsodent." It's remarkable how many of the old jingles and catchphrases are still around. Obviously they worked. TV commercials weren't as much of an annoyance in the 1950s as they are today, when it seems like commercials take up half of the show. In the 1950s, a typical one-hour show included eight minutes of commercials, compared to eighteen minutes today. It's not just your imagination. Commercials take up a lot more time than they used to.

Baby Boomers must have been the cleanest generation in our history, because supermarkets had entire aisles of soap and detergents, and both were heavily advertised on TV. Believe it or not, detergents were not widely available until the 1950s. Prior to the Fifties, soap was used for washing everything, but after WWII, detergents that reduced foam and didn't clabber like soap were developed for washing dishes and clothes in the new automatic washers. By 1953, sales of detergents surpassed those of soap. It wasn't until years later that we realized that some of the chemicals in detergents, such as phosphates, were not very biodegradable and were harmful to the environment. Anyway, our mothers used the detergent, and we used the soap. Soap was just something we used for bathing until we screwed up and let out a four-letter word within earshot of our parents. Then, like Ralphie in *A Christmas Story*, a 1983 movie classic about growing up in the 1950s, we learned what soap tasted like. Ralphie preferred Palmolive, but I can tell you with firsthand knowledge that all soaps were yucky. One soap we used a lot of and never had to eat was Boraxo, a powdered hand soap that washed the crap off your hands but was so abrasive it also took the skin off. I guess we tolerated it partly due to a great TV anthology, *Death Valley Days*, that was sponsored by Borax. We loved the cowboy stories hosted by "The Old Ranger." After the Old Ranger retired in 1965, future president Ronald Reagan hosted the show for a couple of years. I'll bet you didn't know that.

Besides soap, toothpaste and toothbrushes were the other big hygiene products. It wasn't until 1955 that the first American Dental Association-recommended fluoride toothpastes came on the market, with Crest being the first one. Ipana Toothpaste had the best mascot with Bucky Beaver, but the stuff tasted like carbolic acid, and by the mid-1970s it was mercifully gone. Toothbrushes weren't the high-tech whirling, pulsing devices they are today – the first electric toothbrush wasn't on the market until 1959. Fluoridated water was generally accepted as a great advance in preventing tooth decay, but some politicians were convinced it was a Communist plot aimed at destroying the United States.

Cars were selling as fast as Detroit could roll them off the assembly lines during the Fifties. With few exceptions, Americans drove American-made cars. In those postwar years, foreign car manufacturing companies were just getting back on their feet, but it didn't matter much, since American cars were the best-made cars in the world then, and they were big and fast, which is what buyers wanted. By the end of the decade, a few Volkswagen Beetles were showing up on American roads, but most Americans turned up their noses at such a small, underpowered car.

In the Fifties, you paid for purchases with either cash or a check. Credit cards were in their infancy, and the few credit cards available in the early 1950s were issued largely by gasoline companies and department stores. The earliest credit cards weren't actually cards, they were little imprinted metal plates that the merchant ran through an imprinting machine. Some merchants kept the little plates until the customer was in the store and was ready to pay. During the decade, it became possible to use a credit card at different merchants when Diners Club, Carte Blanche, and American Express issued cards. In 1958, Bank of America created the BankAmericard, which eventually evolved into the Visa card. By the end of the decade, credit cards were the familiar plastic cards in use today, although there was no magnetic coding, and the cards had the users' name and address in raised numbers and letters that embossed the information onto charge slips. Until Visa and MasterCard were available and accepted by most merchants, people often carried a dozen or more different cards from department stores, gas companies, and banks. Wallet makers made special accordion-like wallets just for holding credit cards, and people often bragged about how many credit cards they owned, apparently to show what good credit they had. Most credit cards issued in the 1950s required full payment of the balance each month, but by the end of the decade, the concept of revolving accounts was becoming well known, and credit card companies quickly realized that they could boost revenues substantially by requiring minimum payments and charging a high interest rate on the balance.

CHAPTER 8

Gadgets and Gizmos

With scientists and engineers returning to civilian life after the war, the 1950s decade was an explosion of technological advances that brought amazing new products to consumers. Nothing was bigger than television, which existed in a few markets prior to 1950, but by the middle of the decade, most Americans were enjoying the new medium. And they were enjoying it to a degree that no one could have possibly predicted.

Early Fifties TV was nothing like today. TV sets were expensive, the picture was in black and white, and you changed channels with a knob, not a remote control. You could use a "rabbit ears" antenna that sat on top of the set, but to get the best picture quality, you needed to install a large antenna on the roof of your house. Then the antenna had to be rotated to line up with the station, which was impossible, since most cities had three stations (one for each network: ABC, CBS, and NBC), and sometimes a fourth station, a government-operated educational channel. So you settled on a position that would give a halfway decent picture for all channels. Some high-rollers spent the big bucks on a motorized rotating antenna. Electronics magazines were full of articles about the different kinds of antennas, with geeky terms like signal to noise ratio, radiation patterns, and RF gain. Most people just went to the local hardware store and bought whatever the salesperson recommended.

Complicating matters was that TV stations broadcast on Very High Frequency (VHF – channels 2-13) and Ultra High Frequency (UHF – channels 14-69) bands. Television sets had two tuners, one for VHF and one for UHF, and different antennas were needed for each band. In the early years of TV broadcasting, most stations were VHF, but independent stations and some network affiliate stations started popping up on UHF. The UHF tuners were flakey, and it was difficult to get a decent picture and sound. Today most people get TV signals over a cable or satellite dish, so it doesn't matter except to the few people who still pull TV signals from the air with an antenna.

There was no cable or satellite TV transmission. TV signals were transmitted by analog signals sent from tall transmitting towers. If you lived within a few miles of the TV station, you got a decent picture. If you lived further away, you put your TV antenna on a tall mast. If you lived far out in the countryside, which many people still did in the Fifties, you had no TV. Americans got a preview of communications of the future in 1960 when the Echo I satellite was launched into earth orbit. This was an ingenious 100-foot diameter Mylar balloon that was inflated after it was in orbit. With an ultra-thin metallic coating, it was used experimentally to bounce television, radio, and telephone signals to distant receivers. The coolest part was that it was so big that it was easily visible to the naked eye. Newspapers printed times when it would be overhead, and millions of Americans were outside on clear nights watching it pass overhead around sunrise and sunset.

TV sets weren't very reliable in those early years. They were full of vacuum tubes, which generated a lot of heat, and the tubes burned out often. Because the vacuum tubes took a long time to heat up, you waited 30-45 seconds after turning the set on before the picture and sound came on. When tubes burned out, you had two choices. You could call a TV repairman, which by the mid-1950s was a young but flourishing industry, or you could look for a tube that wasn't lighted up, remove it, and replace it yourself. Many drugstores and hardware stores had machines where you could plug in the tube, let it heat up, and a meter would indicate if the tube was good or bad. The machines had several different sockets for different tubes, and if the tube was bad, you could buy a new tube while you were there, take it home and stick it in the TV set, and if you were lucky, it worked. If it didn't work, you went to Plan B and called the repairman. If your TV set was a big cabinet model, it wasn't easy to get in the car, so the repairman came to your house. Unfortunately, TV sets had the maddening habit of coming back to life as soon as the repairman walked through the door, but you still had to pay him for a service call.

Although crude transistors had been first produced in the 1920s, the first commercially useful transistor was developed by British-born American physicist William Shockley in the late 1940s. By the end of the 1950s, radios, TVs, and many other electronic devices were manufactured using transistors instead of vacuum tubes, a huge advance due to the reduced power requirements and heat output of transistors. For the first time, Americans could buy lightweight mobile electronic devices that didn't require heavy short-lived batteries and were the size of a breadbox. And these devices were instant-on, since they had no tubes to heat up. By the end of the decade, it seemed like everyone carried a small transistor radio around with them. Some companies marketed them as "shirt-pocket" radios. Mass production and competition made prices low enough for almost any family to buy several. One of the biggest hit rock 'n' roll songs of 1961 was *Transistor Sister* by singer Freddy Cannon, a clear sign of the popularity of these small portable radios.

The telephone was one device that did not appear to advance very much during the Fifties. AT&T had a longstanding monopoly on telephone service in the US, and they acted like a monopoly. If you wanted telephone service, you went to AT&T. If you wanted a telephone, you bought it from AT&T, and like a Model T Ford, you could get it in any color as long as it was black. Actually, you didn't buy the telephone, you rented it, a little fact that many people never realized. Customers ended up paying hundreds of dollars over the years for a phone that cost only a few dollars to manufacture by Western Electric, the manufacturing subsidiary of AT&T. AT&T was eventually broken up, and today there are many companies competing for telephone service, but in the 1950s, AT&T was the only game in town.

Compared to today, telephone service was crude and expensive. The phones, which had rotary dials (not phased out until the 1970s), were wired into wall outlets, so you couldn't move them from room to room like you can with modular jacks.

There were no cordless phones. If you wanted another phone, you applied to AT&T and waited till they delivered and installed it, then you paid every month for it. Local calling areas were generally small, so if a friend or relative lived more than a few miles away, it was often a long distance call. And direct-dial was not available for long distance calls in most areas until the 1960s. For a long distance call, you dialed "O" to get an operator. You gave the operator the phone number and told her (it was always a woman) if you wanted the call to be station-to-station or person-to-person. Station-to-station meant that when someone answered the phone, the long distance charges began. In a person-to-person call, you specified the name of the person you wanted on the phone. When someone answered the phone, the operator asked for that person, and when the person came on the line, the charges started. Person-to-person calls were considerably more expensive than station-to-station.

Long distance calls were expensive. If you had out-of-town friends or relatives, you could spend a fortune each month on the phone chatting with them. People routinely wrote long letters to each other to avoid long distance phone bills. If you were on vacation, you didn't call your relatives, you sent them a postcard. There was a trick that many people used to avoid the exorbitant charges for long distance. Suppose that your kid was going away to college hundreds of miles away. You wanted to know that the kid got there safely, but you didn't want them to make an expensive long distance call, so you had your kid dial "O" and give your phone number and tell the operator to make it a person-to-person call to Clark Gable or any fictitious name that had been prearranged with your kid. When the operator asked for that person, the parent replied that they weren't at home. It worked like a charm. I'm sure that the operators knew they were being bamboozled, but I doubt if they cared that much, since everyone hated AT&T, and it was gratifying to stick it to them occasionally.

Phone numbers were shorter in the Fifties. In our city, they were only six digits – two letters and four numbers. I still remember the phone number at the first house I lived in:

CR(escent)-2173. Later, a seventh digit was added. Soon after our family moved to the town of Decatur in the mid-1950s, our number was BU(tler) 9-9105. Until direct long distance dialing was available, there were no area codes. Eventually, the letters were replaced with all numbers.

As Atlanta grew, the number of phone lines failed to keep pace. The result was that many people had "party lines," where two or three parties shared a line. Each party had their own distinctive ring, and you were only supposed to pick up the phone on your ring. If you picked up the phone to make a call and one of the other parties was on the line, you heard them talking, and you had to hang up and make your call later. The advantage of a party line was that it was cheaper than having a private line. The disadvantage was that if the other party used the phone a lot, you often couldn't make or receive calls. This occasionally led to heated exchanges between people who shared a line.

There were no cell phones of course, so if you were away from your home and needed to make a call, you stopped at a pay telephone. Pay telephone booths were everywhere, and they were well marked. To use one, you dropped some coins into a slot, got a dial tone, and dialed a number. If the number was busy, your coins were refunded. Having to stop and look for a telephone seems so archaic now, but it's only been the last fifteen years or so that cell phones have been in widespread use.

If there was an emergency, you dialed "O" and described the kind of emergency to the operator, who forwarded your call to the police, fire department, or ambulance service. 9-1-1 service did not begin until 1968, but many communities were very slow to adopt the new number. Even today, some communities do not have 9-1-1 service. In hindsight, this seems strange, since Great Britain has had 9-9-9 telephone service for emergencies since the 1930s.

If you've watched a lot of old movies, you've probably seen scenes where the bad guys, usually kidnappers, would be talking to the good guys on the phone. There were several anxious minutes while telephone company technicians desperately tried to trace the call. Someone in the background would be whispering "Keep them on the line until we trace the call." This seems archaic now when we have the caller's name and phone number pop up instantly on an ID box, but that's the way it was until the last couple of decades.

Amateur radio, which operated over the so called "shortwave" bands, was very popular in the Fifties. Some enthusiasts (called "hams") had transceivers that would broadcast and receive, and many people had receivers only. You could easily recognize the ham radio operators in your neighborhood, since they had big antennas in their yard. Hams have to be licensed by the federal government, but the licensing requirements are less strict today than in the past, when hams had to pass a proficiency test in Morse code, a requirement that was dropped in 2007. In practice, in the Fifties, most amateur radio operators used voice transmission, not Morse code. With a good radio and antenna, a ham could communicate with other hams around the world. In the 1950s, amateur radio operators provided invaluable service by sending and receiving messages to and from remote areas of the world where telephone systems did not exist. Their radio was often the only means of communicating with the outside world that was available to researchers, missionaries, and others who went off the beaten path. When natural disasters struck, hams set up communications networks to coordinate relief efforts. With communications satellites and cell phones today, it's hard to appreciate how valuable amateur radio has been in crisis situations in the past, but amateur radio operators were often the heroes of the day.

Many people were intrigued with shortwave radio but did not want to go through the effort and expense of obtaining a license and buying the expensive gear required for two-way communications. But just searching for radio stations around the world was a fun, inexpensive hobby in those pre-Internet days. A number of companies made cheap shortwave radios. Hallicrafters, now defunct, was the best-known brand, but many people bought a Heathkit shortwave radio kit, which required the owner to assemble the radio. You could save a significant amount of money by buying one of these kits and putting everything together yourself, which required soldering dozens of electronic parts onto circuit boards. I built a Heathkit four-tube superheterodyne (I have no idea what the word means) shortwave receiver and strung a wire antenna to a tree in the backyard. It worked great, and I had many hours of fun wearing a set of headphones and tweaking the tuning dial, trying to pull distant radio stations out of the static.

Electronic kit-building was very popular in the Fifties. Parts had to be individually inserted onto circuit boards, along with a lot of wires, and the labor was a big part of the cost of a manufactured electronic device. You could save a good bit of money if you did the assembly yourself. It saved money, but it was also fun for hobbyists who were handy with a soldering iron. You could get almost anything electronic in a kit, including television sets, radios, stereo receivers and amplifiers, and many other electronic items. By the 1980s, however, separate electronic parts like transistors, capacitors, and resistors were part of integrated circuits, where little assembly was required, so kit-building lost its appeal as it could no longer save much money.

Unlike today, there wasn't much of a range of electronic recording devices available to most people. For sound, there was only reel-to-reel tape, where tape from a reel of magnetic tape was threaded through a set of read-record heads and attached to an empty reel. The sound quality was very high, but the tapes and recording machines were heavy and bulky, and playing something that was on the last part of a tape required forwarding the tape reel for several minutes for a long tape. After playing a tape, the reel then had to be rewound. Small, portable tape recorders like the Dictaphone were available, and these used proprietary tape cartridges, but the sound quality was suitable only for dictation.

Videotape did not come into use until 1956, but the machines for recording and playing videotape were very large and expensive and were developed for use by producers of television shows. Prior to 1956, TV shows were either live, shot by a motion picture camera onto photographic film, or recorded by a kinescope, a crude device that recorded the images from a video monitor onto 16mm or 35mm motion picture film. Videotape was a huge advance over the kinescope. The quality of kinescope recordings was pretty horrible, and if you're seen some of the early shows that were recorded on a kinescope, you know what I mean. But prior to 1956, when networks needed to record and distribute shows that were shot "live," kinescope recordings were the only way.

For listening to music, there was only one choice besides reel-to-reel magnetic tape: phonograph records. Cassette tapes and 8-track cartridges were not introduced until the 1960s. Digital music media would have to wait until the late 1980s. There were three types of phonograph records, classified by their rotation speed on a turntable. The oldest type was 78 rpm, and these were rapidly being phased out in favor of the longer-playing 33⅓ rpm records. The other format was the smaller 45 rpm. The 33⅓ rpm records were used for albums, while the 45 rpm was used for single recordings. Record players made in the 1950s typically had three speeds - 33⅓ rpm, 45 rpm, and 78 rpm - in order to accommodate all three record formats. By the end of the decade, the first transistorized record players were being marketed. These were much lighter than the older vacuum tube models and could be carried from place to place much more easily, a big attraction for teenagers. As the decade ended, stereophonic recordings were being produced, which was a huge advance in music quality.

Quality of home sound systems varied enormously, from cheap portable record players to extremely sophisticated and expensive turntables, amplifiers, and speakers, but all suffered the same weaknesses – records scratched easily, and even with the most expensive systems, the stylus that followed the grooves in the record eventually degraded the sound quality. It was a far cry from the music CDs of today where theoretically a CD can be played millions of times with no loss in sound quality. Fortunately, many of the classic oldies are available today on CDs or digital downloads.

Americans have been avid photographers ever since Eastman Kodak started mass-producing cameras. Americans returning from the war were eager to film their new families from birth through college graduation, and cameras were big sellers in the Fifties. Cameras used film, since digital photography was decades in the future. The most popular cameras used 35 millimeter cartridges or one of the wider roll films. Most of the cameras used by Americans in the 1950s were American-made by companies like Kodak, Ansco, and Argus. Japanese cameras were first brought into the US by Korean War veterans who were stationed in Japan. They were so popular that within a few years, most 35mm cameras sold in the US were Japanese brands like Nikon, Minolta, Pentax, and Canon.

After taking pictures, the film had to be rewound and taken to a developer to have slides or prints made. Some camera stores did film processing, but most people took their exposed film to local drugstores, which sent the film to a processor. It would be the 1970s before mass-market film developing services like the Fotomat drive-through kiosks would exist. It usually took several days to get the finished slides or prints back. Most photography was black and white, since color film was more expensive than black and white both for the film and the processing.

Many people shot color slide film. The disadvantage of slides was that you had to have a slide projector, and projectors were expensive. Kodak was the best known brand, but other companies made cheaper ones. Another disadvantage was for the viewer. If you were at your brother-in-law's house looking at his vacation pictures, you could flip through them as fast as you wanted, but if he was showing slides, you were a captive audience at his mercy.

The Polaroid Land Camera was introduced in 1948, and throughout the 1950s, various models of these cameras were hugely successful. The attraction was obvious: instant pictures, although they were grainy, and the images faded in a short time. Color film was not available until the 1960s. The 1950s models were expensive, but by the early 1970s, Polaroid was introducing very inexpensive models like the "Swinger," and for years afterward, it seemed like everyone had a Polaroid camera. Eventually, one-hour film processing was widely available, and the instant photos of the Polaroid cameras were not as attractive as they once were.

Movie cameras were popular with parents who wanted to record the first steps of their babies and catch them with their strained carrots in mid-drool. The Fifties home movie cameras were relatively crude, with wind-up motors and 8mm or 16mm film that had to be threaded through the camera. There were no zoom lenses either. Super 8 cameras, with easy-to-load cartridges, electric motors, and zoom lenses came along in the early Sixties, but parents in the Fifties shot a lot of film on Standard 8 cameras, to the future dismay of Baby Boomers who were the unwitting subjects.

Raytheon introduced a commercial microwave oven in 1954, but at a price of almost $3,000, there weren't many buyers. Microwave ovens made by the Tappan Stove Company were available in 1955, but they cost about $1,500. The first affordable microwave oven was the Amana Radarange in 1967 which sold for $500, still a lot of money for the time. It would be another decade before microwaves were popping up in a lot of homes. By this time, manufacturers of frozen TV dinners had redesigned their packaging, since the original aluminum trays would have fried microwave ovens.

There were no personal computers in the Fifties. In fact even the smallest computers filled a large room, contained thousands of vacuum tubes, and cost millions of dollars. Personal computers did not exist until the 1970s. Businesses used mechanical machines like typewriters, teletypes, and calculators, although electric typewriters were in wide use by the early 1960s. The sound of clacking typewriters was one that every office worker was familiar with. Calculators were big, heavy mechanical machines made by companies like Friden and Monroe. They were also noisy and slow and jammed often, which required a service technician to come and unjam the gears. Comptometers were an old type of adding machine that was still in use in the Fifties. Teletype machines, also called teleprinters, were used for typewritten communications over dedicated telephone lines. These were used mainly by large businesses. Teletypes were made largely obsolete by the introduction of fax machines in the 1970s.

Photocopying machines made by Xerox weren't widely available and affordable until the early 1960s. In the 1950s, copies were made by using carbon paper while typing, but this was limited to only one copy, which went into the office files. Even today, some typists use the archaic "cc" (carbon copy) to indicate that copies of a document have been sent to others, although the more modern term "xc" is often used.

When multiple copies had to be made, mimeograph machines were used. These machines were most often used to produce materials for institutions, such as examinations for schools and Sunday bulletins for churches. The process was very simple. Waxed sheets of special paper were used for stencils. Writing or typing on the stencil created a master that was attached to an ink-filled cylinder. When the drum was turned, ink flowed through the parts of the master that had been cut by a stylus or typewriter, and blank paper sheets fed through the machine picked up the ink. The cheapest machines were hand-operated, but the more expensive electric mimeographs were faster. No one who went to school in the 1950s will ever forget the peculiarly addicting smell of a mimeographed exam, especially when it was freshly printed. I read somewhere that the ink had alcohol in it, so maybe we got a little buzz from it. With all the hassle and messiness involved, mimeograph machines were joyfully tossed aside when photocopiers became available.

I can't end this chapter without mentioning the greatest technological triumph of the decade: Silly Putty. The General Electric engineer who created the stuff from boric acid and silicone oil while trying to develop a synthetic rubber called it "Gupp." Since GE couldn't think of a use for the stuff, one of their engineers gave some to a toy store owner, who, since Easter was coming, packaged it in a plastic egg and marketed it as Silly Putty. At least that's how one story goes.

The 1950s was a decade of huge technological advances, but many developments in science, engineering, and medicine would not result in marketable products and services till the next decade. Still, we got a good preview of the future during the 1950s.

CHAPTER 9

Food, Glorious Food

Few people went hungry in the 1950s. Parents, remembering the Great Depression when many people did go hungry, made sure that pantries and refrigerators were kept full. With huge chain supermarkets opening throughout the decade, shoppers were offered almost bewildering choices of foods all in one store. The supermarkets of the Fifties didn't have all the amenities that today's supermarkets have, but they were a far cry from the small corner grocery stores our parents had grown up with.

There were two products, however, that most Americans did not buy at a supermarket: milk and bread. These were delivered right to your door a couple of mornings each week. Dairies delivered milk and cream early in the morning before most people were even awake. The dairy truck was not refrigerated, so they surrounded the milk with cardboard cartons of dry ice, which is frozen carbon dioxide. If a kid got up early and begged, the milkman might give him a little piece of the dry ice, which was fun to play with. Before our mother went to bed the night before, she would leave our empty glass bottles on the front porch. In one of the bottles she had dropped enough change to pay for the milk, with a note if she wanted anything different from our usual delivery. The milkman came, took the empties and the money, and he left the milk. The glass milk bottles had foil caps crimped over the top. I sometimes took a full bottle out of the refrigerator (which my mother always called the icebox, which is what she grew up with) and noticed that the foil wasn't crimped very tightly and that it came off very easily. Many years later my mother told me that to save money, she poured the fresh whole milk into a big bowl, mixed up an equal amount of milk made from powdered milk, then mixed the two and poured it into milk bottles. This also explained why there were more bottles in the refrigerator than were on the porch – she had some extras.

Bread and pastries were delivered by the bakery truck a couple of times a week. The bakery truck came later in the morning, so that the lady of the house could pick out what she wanted from the big tray the bakery man brought to the door. You could get bread, cakes, and pastries, and it was fresh from the oven, so it smelled so tantalizing. In the summer, my sisters and I were out of school, and our mother would let us pick out our favorite cookies. Eventually the dairies started buying each other out and consolidating, the same with the bakeries, so they no longer needed to home-deliver to be competitive. In Atlanta, by the end of the decade, dairies and bakeries were wholesaling their products to supermarkets, and home deliveries ended, along with a quaint custom started by bakeries – the "Baker's Dozen." In a bakery, when you bought a dozen cookies or donuts or any kind of pastry, you got an extra one free. In the big, impersonal supermarkets, that custom died.

Occasionally my family had special meals we called "Derailment Dinners." My father worked for a railroad company. Once in a while, a freight train would derail. Sometimes canned foods were being shipped on these trains. Since the cans got dented or dirty or were even underwater, they could not be sold to the stores they were being shipped to. As part of the insurance settlement, the railroad was allowed to sell these canned goods to employees for two cents a can, but the labels had to be removed first, and the cans could only be marked "F" for fruits or "V" for vegetables. The stuff was dirt cheap, but you never knew what you were going to get until you opened the can. On "Derailment Dinner" night, my mother would open some cans of fruits and vegetables, plus some bread, and that was dinner. It gave a whole new meaning to the phrase "pot luck."

But most food and drinks came from the supermarket. As a large family, we guzzled soft drinks, so we bought Coca-Colas by the case. Throughout most of the Fifties, Cokes came only in little 6½-oz bottles, and you bought them in a six-bottle cardboard carton or in a heavy wooden case that held twenty-four bottles. They were returnable bottles, and when you went into the supermarket, you took your empties to the front of the store, where they gave you a credit slip for two cents a bottle. After you filled your cart with groceries you went to the cash register and turned in the bottle credit slip and the cashier took it off the total. The two cents deposit on bottles was a great money-maker for kids. Many times, people would toss the bottles alongside a road. Kids would pick them up, and when they had a load of them, they took them to a grocery store and got their reward. A lot of kids got their spending money that way. By the way, the bottles were not recycled as we use the word today. Instead of being melted down and made into new glass, they were cleaned and reused by the soft drink bottlers.

I mentioned Coca-Cola because that was our favorite drink. There were others, of course, including many of the brands that are popular today, but most soft drinks were colas or citrus drinks, and there were no diet colas until 1958 (Coca-Cola's first diet drink was Tab, introduced in 1963). And just for the record, Cokes had real sugar in them, not the "high fructose corn syrup" imitation the modern ones have. There's a difference. Note to Coke: Give us back our sugar!

Soft drink vending machines were everywhere in the Fifties. They were all designed to dispense bottles, since cans were not introduced until the early Sixties. In the early Fifties, the price was five cents. The next price increase was to six cents, which required every vending machine to be modified to accept pennies. With the inflation of the late-1950s, however, six cents didn't last long, and by the end of the decade, the price was a dime. By this time, many mothers decided to switch their kids to Kool-Aid, since it was a lot cheaper.

Most soft drinks and beer came only in glass bottles until the late 1950s or early 1960s. By the early Sixties, cans (steel at first, but eventually aluminum) were becoming more popular for both consumers and sellers, largely because cans were lighter and took up less space on store shelves. The earliest canned drinks had to be opened with a can opener, which was similar to a bottle opener, but with a sharp point. Can openers were euphemistically and irreverently referred to as "church keys." By the mid-Sixties, cans had pull-tabs, but these were the kind that came completely off the can. It wasn't until the early 1980s that the levered pull-tab that stayed on the can was in wide use. But in the Fifties, most drinks were in bottles, and every home had a metal bottle opener screwed to the cabinets under the countertop in the kitchen.

There were some convenience foods in the supermarkets of the Fifties, but not remotely the variety found today. Rice-A-Roni was introduced in 1958, but kids wouldn't get to say "And I hay-elped" with Shake 'n Bake until 1965. Even further in the future, Hamburger Helper wouldn't be along until the 1970s. Canned soups, vegetables, and fruits made it easier for mothers to fix a meal quickly, and there were some frozen foods too, but most meals were made largely from scratch. Every mother (well, most of them) knew how to make biscuits, cornbread, waffles, pancakes, cakes, pies, and cookies from the basic ingredients of flour, baking powder, baking soda, salt, and sugar. It seems like half the commercials on TV were for White Lily and Gold Medal flours. Flour and other baking products were used so much for home baking that they occupied most of a long row in supermarkets. My mom baked fluffy hot biscuits from scratch practically every morning and evening, as well as turning out some of the world's tastiest cakes and pies. Loaf bread was one of the few baked items she didn't make, but she made some killer cornbread in an ancient cast iron skillet.

Kids love candy, and Baby Boomers were no exception. Our parents grew up in an era when even a single piece of candy was an occasional treat, so they indulged us, probably too much considering how many dentists we kept in business. By the 1950s, most candy sold in stores was commercially manufactured, wrapped, and shipped all over the country, although there were still a lot of small, local candy makers. We had a huge variety of candies to choose from. Surprisingly, although there are many more candies available today, most of our 1950s favorites are still popular, candies like the Hershey Bar, Baby Ruth, Almond Joy, Tootsie Roll, and M&Ms. One that I really miss is the Mason Mint, a round, chocolate-covered mint patty. They were similar to a York Peppermint Patty, but they had a mintier taste that really exploded in your mouth. If you didn't have a nickel for a candy bar, you could settle for the wonderful penny candies like Mary Janes, Bit-O-Honey, and my own favorite, Peanut Butter Logs. A lot of the penny candies are still made today, but they cost a lot more than a penny.

One of our favorite treats was Cracker Jack, a snack consisting of caramel-coated popcorn and peanuts that almost everyone loved. It was an American tradition dating back to the late 19th century and was very popular at baseball games as evidenced by the line "Buy me some peanuts and Cracker Jack, I don't care if I never get back" in the song "Take me Out to the Ball Game." Cracker Jack came in a cardboard box and had a "toy surprise" inside. For kids, half the fun of Cracker Jack was seeing what kind of chintzy little trinket was inside. Today, it's hard to find Cracker Jack in the box. Most stores sell it in a bag, and there's no toy surprise inside. I recently found a bin full of Cracker Jack boxes in a drugstore, and I bought every box. But it's not the same now. The box just says "Surprise Inside," and the surprise is just a little slip of paper with a joke or a riddle.

And how can I talk about treats without mentioning Peeps. These disgusting little marshmallow candies, introduced in 1958, are shaped like chicks, bunnies and other animals. Millions of Peeps are sold every year, mainly to fill Easter baskets, but no one has ever actually been seen eating one. Well, that's not exactly true. My sister Jean conned her husband John into competing in a Peeps-eating contest a couple of years ago. He ate enough Peeps to win the contest and get some choice concert tickets, but he'll never make that mistake again. Just to remind him of the debacle, I send him a few boxes of Peeps every Easter.

There weren't a lot of restaurants in Atlanta in the post-war years, and the ones we had were mostly one-of-a-kind local eateries. Franchised fast-food restaurants and drive-throughs didn't start showing up in Atlanta until the 1960s. Neither did the big restaurant chains exist in our area in those days. We did have a lot of "greasy spoon" diners and mom and pop restaurants.

These were fun places to eat, since they usually had great hot dogs, hamburgers, and grilled cheese sandwiches for us kids. And if you sat at a booth, there was a box on the wall with all the jukebox selections. You dropped a coin in the slot, pushed the button for your song, then the kids rushed over to the big jukebox with flashing lights and watched as it flipped the right 45-rpm record onto a turntable and played it.

There was one kind of restaurant that we did have in the South, and people swore by their favorite. Barbecue wasn't just food, it was manna from heaven, a clear sign that God loved us and wanted us to be happy. In the South, barbecue was synonymous with pig, although misguided souls who preferred beef (Texans) or chicken (Yankees) were tolerated, ignorant as they were. One of the first barbecue restaurant chains in Georgia, the Old Hickory House, was very popular and still operates a couple of restaurants in Atlanta. It is said that Jimmy Carter, when he was President, had Old Hickory House barbecue shipped to the White House. I don't know about that, but the barbecue was mighty good. Old Hickory House was not the only barbecue restaurant by any means. There were, and still are, dozens of them in the Atlanta area, many of them just hole-in-the-wall places serving some of the best barbecue in the world. One thing is for sure, a lot of pigs have given their lives for a worthy cause.

Southerners also loved fish, and every mom-and-pop diner served fried catfish and sometimes fried ocean perch. Fried catfish and hushpuppies were delicacies to us. Today, restaurants serve fish grilled, baked, broiled, and blackened, but that's for Yankees. The only true way to cook fish is to roll it in cornmeal and cook it in fat. Any other way is an insult to the fish. In Georgia, we had a chain of fish restaurants called Rio Vista, where you had all-you-can-eat fried catfish, ocean perch, and chicken. Some of the most satisfying and gut-busting meals I had as a kid were at Rio Vista. In the 1970s, Red Lobster came along and put a lot of seafood restaurants out of business. Red Lobster is very good, but their cheese biscuits just aren't the same as hushpuppies.

Eating at a restaurant was a special treat for us though, and it didn't happen very often. Like most families we knew, we weren't poor, but there wasn't a lot of money for extravagances like eating out at restaurants. Most of the time we ate at home, which was no hardship, since most mothers were marvelous cooks. Almost every home had several thick cookbooks, including the mother of them all, *Betty Crocker's Picture Cook Book*. They must have had some great photographers, because the food our mothers whipped up from those recipes never looked as colorful or appetizing as the pictures in the books! Another popular cookbook was *The Joy of Cooking*, and if your mother was way ahead of the curve, she might have a copy of *The Alice B. Toklas Cookbook*, published in 1954, which included the famous recipe for cannabis brownies.

Almost as soon as television became a part of our lives, TV cooking shows popped up on many local stations. They weren't very sophisticated, certainly nothing like the shows on The Food Network today, and the cooks weren't as sizzling hot as Rachel Ray, but many of our mothers watched them religiously. Most cooking shows were aired on weekday mornings while we were in school, but if we were home we sometimes watched them with our mothers. Actually, they could be fun to watch. Since they were live, you saw all the boo-boos that are edited out on videotaped shows today. TV cooking shows gradually became more elaborate and sophisticated, with colorful kitchens and higher production values, but in those early years, it was just a lady cooking food in a chintzy-looking TV studio kitchen. And with black and white TV, the food looked pretty bland. Julia Child would revolutionize TV cooking shows with *The French Chef* series, but that would be in the next decade.

In the Fifties, there weren't many ethnic restaurants except in big cities with large immigrant populations. Atlanta wasn't one of those cities, and it was virtually impossible to find even a pizzeria or Tex-Mex restaurant, which are everywhere now. Frozen pizzas were hardly known in the period, and the ones available tasted like cardboard with a bit of cheese and a smear of really gross tomato sauce. We loved to get Chef Boy-Ar-Dee pizza-making kits from the supermarket. Everything except the meat came in one box: the flour, grated cheese, and sauce. The best thing is that kids could make it themselves. You just mixed the flour with water, then spread the dough out in a rectangular baking pan (I doubt if you could find a real pizza pan in Atlanta then), poured on the sauce, and sprinkled the cheese on top. If you wanted to, you could add your own meat. What came out of the oven a few minutes later wasn't real pizza by any stretch of the imagination, but kids loved it. Chef Boy-Ar-Dee also made an everything-in-one-box spaghetti dinner ("A delicious, nourishing meal in only 12 minutes"), and they vigorously promoted their pizza and spaghetti dinners in TV commercials featuring a cheesy (sorry, no pun intended) Chef Boy-Ar-Dee with a really bad phony Italian accent.

One of our least favorite dinners was salmon croquettes, which our mom, in a rare display of cruelty and child abuse, made at least twice a month. These were really gross. You took canned salmon – the cheapest brand, with pieces of bone and skin – and mixed it with eggs and stale bread crumbs and mashed out the croquettes. After our mom baked these abominations, we had to eat them. They were so foul that only squeezing lemon juice and a lot of ketchup on them made them edible, and just barely at that. Compared to canned salmon, fish sticks are gourmet food, minced pollock at its finest. The only redeeming quality for salmon was that it's loaded with Omega-3 fatty acids, though we had never heard of them at the time. Yes, I know salmon is considered a delicacy, but the canned stuff we ate was barely fit for cat food, much less humans.

Dessert was usually our favorite part of dinner (which we called supper). Our mom made desserts that would make any restaurant's pastry chef envious. Her cakes and pies were legendary. She baked cakes and pies from scratch, and that meant sifting flour, grating chocolate or coconut with a hand grater; making the flakiest pie crusts with real butter; and using fresh fruits like blackberries, apples, and cherries. Then she baked them in a small gas oven in a tiny kitchen that got to be stifling hot in our un-air-conditioned house. I can still taste the melt-in-your-mouth goodness. During the hottest part of summer, she would sometimes give herself a break and make Jell-O salad with canned fruits. One easy-to-make dessert was Dromedary Canned Date Bread. Yes, canned. It was a moist, dark, semi-sweet bread chock full of chopped dates and walnuts. Slice off a piece, spread a little cream cheese or butter on it, and it was heaven. Cake-in-a-can may not sound that appetizing, but it's one of those things you had to be there to understand. You can't get it today, but there are recipes for it and even a packaged mix that alleges to produce the same results. I haven't tried making it, but I can't imagine it would be as tasty or as filling as the original stuff in a can.

I mentioned cream cheese and butter, which were staples for us. Margarine was often used in the Fifties instead of butter, but butter — let's face it — tastes better. In any case, there was no concept of spreadable cream cheese, butter, or margarine. You kept the stuff in the refrigerator, and it was hard as a rock. Trying to spread it on the soft white bread of that era resulted only in demolishing the bread. So you cut off a piece, let it warm up a bit outside the refrigerator, then softened it up more with a spoon before you could spread it on anything. Cream cheese, butter, and margarine came in foil-wrapped "bricks," not the tubs that the spreadable kinds come in today.

Yes, we consumed butter with reckless abandon, blissfully unaware of words like "cholesterol" and "saturated fats." And vegetables were cooked in lard, which is just a polite term for pig fat. Shortening, which was made from vegetable oil, was healthier and was used in baking, but lard made the best French fries, which was all that mattered to us in those less health-conscious times. Salt was another thing we didn't worry about too much. If it wasn't tasty enough, pour on the salt. The phrase "salt to taste" was standard cookbook text. In the Fifties, a salt substitute, MSG (monosodium glutamate) began showing up in American supermarkets. American military personnel stationed in Japan after the war had discovered MSG in Japanese food and loved it. Soon MSG, packaged as "Accent," was the rage across America.

With its motto "wakes up food flavor," it was advertised as a substitute for salt (sodium chloride), and virtually every home had a bottle. We loved the stuff, it was like a miracle for improving the taste of meats and vegetables. It was only later that we realized that MSG was not good for you, and the phrase "Chinese Restaurant Syndrome" was coined for the headaches and other ailments that MSG caused.

Duodenal ulcers were fairly common in adults during this period, much more so than today. One day in 1956, my dad was carried from his office in an ambulance to the nearest hospital emergency room, which fortunately was less than a mile away. They thought he was having a heart attack, but tests showed he had an ulcer. In those days it was thought that a spicy, rich diet caused ulcers, so doctors prescribed a very bland diet of stuff like milk and saltines, not learning until decades later that many ulcers are caused by bacteria and that diet has little effect in causing or curing ulcers. Unfortunately, millions of people like my dad gave up many of his favorite foods needlessly.

I remember grilled cheese sandwiches as one of our favorite things to make at home. Everyone had a heavy steel waffle iron (next to toasters, they were the gift most often given to newlyweds). Making waffles was an exercise in frustration, since there was no such thing as Teflon coatings, and we didn't have no-stick sprays either. We loved waffles, but our parents didn't make them very often, since the waffles stuck to the plates, and by the time you scraped them off, they were burned or shredded up or both. But a grilled cheese sandwich, that was a different matter, since you could pop out the waffle plates and use the flat plates. A little butter would grease the plates, then you buttered up the bread and stuck some cheddar cheese in the bread and closed the plate. In a couple of minutes, the cheese was melting onto the hot plate and turning crispy. This was one of the few diner or dime store lunch counter foods that you could make at home that was just as good as eating out.

Like kids everywhere, we loved ice cream with a passion. During the warm months, the "ice cream man" would come down the street a couple of afternoons a week. In the suburbs, he drove a truck; in the city, he rode a three-wheeled bicycle with an insulated cooler on the back. Either way, he drove very slowly down the street with bells jingling or music playing. If your mom was in a good mood, she would give you enough change to run out and get an ice cream. There were all kinds of ice cream, but the favorites were popsicles, Eskimo Pies, fudgesicles, ice cream sandwiches, and my favorite, Drumsticks, which were waffle cones filled with ice cream and topped with chocolate and nuts. Oh boy, those were good, especially on a hot day. Even if your mom was in a good mood and feeling generous, you couldn't count on getting ice cream money more than a couple of times a month, so we made our own popsicles by pouring Kool-Aid into Tupperware popsicle molds and freezing them. It was cheap, and the homemade popsicles were almost as good as the ice cream man's.

Another occasional treat was going to the drugstore (also called a pharmacy). Drugstores weren't as big or as much fun as dime stores, but dime stores were downtown and drugstores were just down the street. The magic of drugstores was the soda fountain, where you could get anything from a Coke to a sandwich. They had the best cherry Cokes in the world, where the soda jerk added maraschino cherry juice right into the still-fizzing Coke. Oh lordy, those were good, light years better than the canned cherry Cokes today. And they had ice cream cones (vanilla, chocolate, or strawberry), milkshakes, malted milk, Coke floats, ice cream sundaes, banana splits, chocolate milk, lime rickeys, whatever you wanted, they made it. The drugstore soda fountain was a place where your sweet dreams came true.

CHAPTER 10

Transportation and Travel

The 1950s had an explosion of transportation and travel options. Although passenger railroad service declined in the 1950s, the proliferation of cars and improved highways allowed Americans to drive long distances for business or pleasure. Ocean liners still plied the oceans, but airplanes were carrying more and more people, and by the end of the decade, jet aircraft were in service. Prosperous Americans were eager to see their country's scenic treasures, and increasing numbers of them paid their way to go overseas to places that had known only war just a few years earlier.

For many decades, passenger rail service was the primary travel mode for Americans traveling to cities more than a few miles away. However, passenger rail travel began declining by the 1920s, as motorized vehicles became available and cheap, and roads were improved to serve cars and trucks. There was a huge increase in rail travel during World War II, but afterward, the decline continued. By 1950, passenger rail service was a shadow of what it had been in 1920. Nevertheless, it was still possible to travel throughout the United States by rail, and our family took advantage of this, since my father worked for a railroad company and we could travel for free. I remember two vacations we took, to Miami and Jacksonville, in the mid-1950s. The sleeping compartment was small, but at night a porter would come around and make up the drop-down beds. I've never slept so well, with the rhythmic clickety-clack of the train wheels (that went away soon afterward, as the railroads went to continuously-welded tracks with no joints). The dining car was a marvelous place where we ate on fine china, used real silverware, and leaned on linen tablecloths while watching the countryside pass by. Dining cars had real kitchens where chefs prepared food as good as any restaurant. Rail travel was an adventure, one that, sadly, most kids today will never know.

At the beginning of the 1950s decade, many railroad locomotives were still steam powered. Diesel-electric locomotives had been introduced shortly before World War II, but the war delayed dieselization, and it was not until 1960 that the last steam locomotives used by the larger railroads were retired from service. It was a great step forward for modernization, but a lot of people miss those old steam engines, as evidenced by the popularity of steam excursion trains all around the country today.

People stopped riding trains because they had cars, a lot of cars. Once the automobile manufacturers retooled their assembly lines from making tanks and airplanes for the war, they started cranking out passenger cars in record numbers. General Motors, Ford, and Chrysler were the big three automobile manufacturers in the Fifties, but other companies were selling cars too, including Nash, which became AMC in 1954 and was ultimately bought by Chrysler; and Packard, which bought Studebaker in 1954, but by the end of the decade, almost all automobiles sold in the United States were built by the big three. Passenger cars were the most popular vehicles sold in the 1950s. Pickup trucks were popular with workmen and farmers. For families, the station wagon was the equivalent of a minivan today. The ultimate station wagon was the "woodie," which originally had real wooden panels on the sides, but eventually the wood was replaced by steel and vinyl that simulated wood. Real woodies are collectors items today, but I don't know if I want a car that could have a termite problem. At the end of the decade, a Corvette sold for less than $4,000 brand new, and a Cadillac Eldorado, the most luxurious American-made car you could buy, cost a bit over $13,000, more than a Rolls-Royce Silver Cloud. Hopefully you didn't buy a Ford Edsel, which was introduced in 1957 and was a colossal flop with its "horsecollar" grille that resembled a woman's genitalia. Cars were supposed to be sexy, but that was going a bit too far.

Suddenly everyone wanted to "see the USA in their Chevrolet," as the advertising jingle went. Cross country travel increased explosively as Americans wanted to see the Grand

Canyon, Yosemite, Yellowstone, and the other national parks that they had heretofore only read about or seen in travelogues. The supporting infrastructure wasn't ready, but entrepreneurs quickly started building hotels, motels, and restaurants along major routes and around tourist attractions. State and local governments started road improvement programs, funded largely by taxes on motor fuels and tires. One of President Eisenhower's major accomplishments was the passage of the "National Interstate and Defense Highways Act of 1956," which authorized and funded a huge network of limited access highways connecting major US cities. The Interstate Highway System became the largest public works project in history. Such huge amounts of money were justified by politicians by linking national defense with the transportation system, which is why the word "Defense" is in the bill's name. Even today, Interstate Highway bridges are required to be designed to carry military loads. With the new Interstate Highways being built and older state highways being widened and improved, millions of Americans were enjoying being able to travel long distances at high speed. And when they needed gasoline, a restaurant, or a place to stay overnight, the facilities were there. A number of major motel chains such as Best Western (1946), Holiday Inn (1952), and Ramada Inn (1954) were born in the postwar years as cross-country travel increased. Seeing the future of travel, many of the new motels were built at Interstate Highway interchanges or on major state highways. There were still plenty of independent mom-and-pop motels, but these declined as travelers went for the newer chain motels, and many of these older motels were on highways that were bypassed by the new Interstate Highways. Even today, you can drive on these old roads and see the remains of businesses and sometimes entire towns that died decades ago.

One of the fun parts of traveling cross-country were the Burma-Shave signs. Burma-Shave was a brand of shaving cream. To advertise the product, the Burma-Vita Company posted humorous rhyming poems on consecutive highway billboard signs spaced a few hundred feet apart. At one time in the 1950s there were an estimated 7,000 of these signs across the United

States. Rhymes went like this: *If daisies / Are your / Favorite flower / Keep pushin' up those / Miles per hour / Burma-Shave.* The Burma-Shave signs are all gone now, but Baby Boomers and their parents remember them fondly from their driving trips.

It's a wonder that we didn't kill ourselves driving in the Fifties. Cars did not have seatbelts, and child car seats were designed only to hold kids in place, not protect them in an accident. Cars didn't have antilock brakes, collapsible steering columns, or reinforced doors, and air bags were unheard of in that era. Somehow we survived, most of us. And it was probably the last decade you could pick up a hitchhiker without fear of having your throat cut.

Some travelers carried their own lodging with them. Recreational vehicles (RVs) had been invented in the 1920s but didn't really have a big market until after World War II. Most of the companies that made RVs before the war went out of business due to a lack of customers and the shortage of aluminum, but Airstream survived, and their shiny aluminum Airstream Clipper was a common sight in campgrounds and RV parks during the Fifties. Winnebago went into business in 1958, but their first models didn't come off the assembly line until the mid-1960s. Camping was popular, but there weren't enough campgrounds around popular tourist sites to handle the crunch brought about by so many families cruising about the country in their cars. Many campgrounds had few if any facilities, so you just pitched a tent, cut some firewood, and hauled water from a nearby lake or stream. Unless you knew the water was safe, you made sure by dropping in some halazone purification tablets and waiting an hour. Today, this kind of camping is called "primitive camping," since camping out has a whole different meaning to most people today.

Even with the highway improvements that were going on during the decade, there were many miles of unpaved roads in the US, even in some urban areas. Some of these were improved with crushed stone and were well maintained, but many were just narrow dirt roads filled with potholes. Flat tires were common, and in rainy weather, dirt roads were virtually impassable. In good weather, the dust could make it impossible to see. Either way, after driving one of these roads, you had to wash your car, and there were very few automatic car washes in those days, so you probably washed your car at home with a hose, a bucket of hot soapy water, and a sponge.

The number of service stations increased too, and most of them were really service stations, doing minor repairs, tune-ups, fixing flat tires, and changing oil as well as selling gas. And they were all what are called "full service" stations today. An attendant pumped your gas, checked the oil, put air in your tires, and wiped your windshield while you sat in your car. Gasoline was leaded, meaning that Tetra-ethyl lead had been added to the gasoline, since many car engines required this to prevent knocking. It was common to hear a driver pull into a service station and say "Fill 'er up with ethyl." Service stations sprang up everywhere during the decade, and a busy intersection might have stations on at least two corners. Stations often had price wars, cutting the price of a gallon of gas till they were barely breaking even. They sometimes had free giveaways for filling up your car. Drinking glasses were a very popular item, and many families probably didn't buy glasses for years. Stations also had a lot of sweepstakes drawings for prizes like barbecue grills and kids' toys, anything to build loyal customers.

Service stations were a handy place to get flat tires repaired or to buy new tires when the old ones were beyond repair. This was important because tires in the 1950s weren't nearly as durable as today, and with the poor condition of many roads, flat tires were inevitable and not an uncommon experience. Tires were typically made with rayon cord. It wasn't until the Sixties that radial belted tires were widely available, and not until the Seventies that steel belted radials were available. Also, tubeless tires like we drive on today would not be widely available until the Sixties. Tubeless tires generally lose air slowly after being punctured. Not so with a tubed tire. You could actually hear a blowout when it happened, and within a very few seconds, you had no tire pressure and could lose control of the car. We take it for granted today that our tires will last for tens of thousands of miles without wearing out or having a flat, but drivers in the Fifties knew better, and "We fix flats" signs were on every service station.

In the cities, many people rode buses, trolleys, and streetcars. Streetcars, also called street railways, had steel wheels that ran on tracks. They were powered by overhead electrical transmission lines, with the car connected to the lines by a spring-loaded rod with a pulley-like trolley that ran along the transmission line. By 1950, cities were expanding rapidly and outgrowing the streetcar lines. Because of the expense of extending the lines, streetcars gave way to rubber-tired trolleys, also called trackless trolleys, that used the same overhead lines. You could tell instantly if a city had trolleys. Downtown intersections had huge spider webs of trolley wires overhead, a sight that people who didn't live back then could hardly imagine today. Eventually the old streetcar tracks were removed or paved over, and streetcars were forgotten. In Atlanta, the last streetcars were retired in 1949 and were sold to South Korea, where they served until the mid-1960s. With the streetcars now gone, mass transit in most US cities consisted of rubber-tired electric trolleys and diesel-powered buses. In Atlanta, the rubber-tired electric trolleys were retired in 1963, and afterwards, Atlanta had an all-bus system, a move that was considered progressive at the time, but in hindsight looks like a poor decision, since many cities are going back to electrical-powered streetcars and trolleys today.

As passenger railroad service declined, intercity bus companies declined also, due to the rise in personal automobile travel. The two biggest intercity bus companies, Greyhound and Trailways, are still operating, but with only a fraction of the ridership they had fifty years ago. In rural areas, Greyhound and Trailways were often used to ship parcels. The sender would take their parcel to the nearest bus station, pay the shipping cost, and the recipient would be notified to pick up the parcel from the receiving station. This was an invaluable service for areas where the nearest post office was many miles away, as it often was, in the days before parcel services like UPS and FedEx were around.

In the early-1950s, virtually all Americans who traveled across the ocean went by ocean liner. The busiest route for liners was on the North Atlantic with ships traveling between Europe and North America. Many countries had ocean liner companies, and it was a matter of national pride to have the biggest, fastest, and most luxurious ships. It was a tradition for American school teachers to travel to Europe on their summer vacation. I remember sitting through their slide shows when school was back in the fall. The most famous ship accident of the era was the sinking of the Italian liner Andrea Doria after colliding with the Swedish liner Stockholm off the coast from Nantucket, Massachusetts in 1956. The Andrea Doria was the last major transatlantic passenger vessel to sink before aircraft became the preferred method of travel. By the early 1970s, only one ocean liner remained on the transatlantic route, as the speed of crossing the ocean became more important than the style of crossing it.

By the end of the Fifties, air travel was the preferred mode of traveling long distances for both domestic and foreign travel. There were many more airlines then, but many of these have merged with other airlines or gone out of business. Some of the bigger airlines that no longer exist are Capital Airlines (merged with United Airlines), Braniff Airways (bankruptcy), and Eastern Airlines (bankruptcy). The primary airlines flying from the US to Europe were TWA (acquired by American Airlines in 2001) and Pan American World Airways (bankruptcy in 1991), better known as Pan Am. For transpacific routes, the major carriers were Pan Am and Northwest Orient Airlines (later renamed Northwest Airlines and later merged with Delta Air Lines).

Until the late Fifties, airlines flew propeller aircraft such as the Boeing Stratocruiser, based on the design of the B-29 bomber; the Lockheed Constellation, one of the most beautiful airplanes ever built; and the Douglas DC-6. The Lockheed Electra was a popular turboprop aircraft. None of these planes had the range to travel from New York to western European cities, so stopovers for refueling were made in places like Gander, Newfoundland and Shannon, Ireland. In 1949, the British-made de Havilland Comet was the first jet aircraft to go into scheduled airline service, but a series of crashes due to a design flaw caused the plane to be taken out of service until the flaw was corrected, and afterwards few people wanted to fly on a plane with such a bad record. In 1958, American-made jet airliners came into service with the Boeing 707 and the Douglas DC-8. General Dynamics produced its first jet airliner, the Convair 880, in 1959, but it was a commercial failure.

For the first time, Europe became an affordable vacation for many Americans. With modern aircraft reducing the travel time to cross the Atlantic from days to hours, Americans also had the time. Europe was still recovering from the war, so things were cheap – really cheap – and the US Dollar was king. In 1957, Arthur Frommer, while in the U.S. Army, wrote a travel guide for American GIs in Europe, and then produced a civilian version called *Europe on $5 a Day*. The book ranked popular landmarks and sights in order of importance and included suggestions on how to travel around Europe on a budget. It was the first travel guide to show Americans that they could afford to travel in Europe. It was a new concept for the time and has been credited with opening the door to modern tourism and travel guidebook publishing, particularly for budget travel.

The 1950s was the first decade that huge numbers of Americans traveled for recreation. We were natural born tourists, always wanting to see what's around the bend. We could be loud and boisterous sometimes, and it was during this decade that the phrase "Ugly American" was coined, but we didn't care. The world was our oyster, and we saw as much of it as we could. It's sad to think now that many of the places we traveled to in those days are too dangerous to visit now with terrorism and civil wars raging.

CHAPTER 11

On the Road to Equality

One of the greatest stage musicals of the decade was *South Pacific*, based on short stories written by James Michener, who had served in the South Pacific during World War II. Premiering in 1949, the show has been ultra successful and is still performed regularly today. With its two intertwined stories of interracial love, audiences of today probably have little appreciation of how controversial the topic was in the racially segregated 1950s. One story involved a love affair between Nellie Forbush, a naïve young nurse from Little Rock, Arkansas, and Emile De Becque, a French planter. The other love story was about Navy Lieutenant Joe Cable and Liat, a Tonkinese girl. Nellie is deeply in love with Emile until she learns that his two dark-skinned children were by a Polynesian woman, which, with Nellie's deep-seated racial prejudices, she cannot accept. Joe Cable, a proper Philadelphian, loves Liat, but he knows that she will not be accepted in his high-society circles at home. Joe is killed on a coast-watching mission, which resolves this issue. Nellie's love for Emile eventually brings her to accept him and his children. Before Joe's death, Emile asks Joe why he and Nellie have such prejudices. Joe replies bitterly in one of the show's most dramatic songs, "Carefully Taught," that people are not born with prejudice, they have to be carefully taught.

And carefully taught we were. Now don't get me wrong. Our parents weren't intentionally mean or hateful, they were simply passing along the racial prejudices and stereotypes that they and generations before them had been taught. That doesn't make it right, that's just the way it was. Our parents did not teach us to hate people of other races, but they genuinely believed that whites were superior to other races. I'm talking about other races in general, but for those of us in the South, "other races" included black people and anyone with darker skin than ours. Atlanta, like many Southern cities, had a large black population, but black people were largely invisible to whites. We saw them, yes, but we didn't mix with them, we didn't go to school with them, we didn't dine with them, we didn't go to church with them, we didn't go to movies with them, we didn't use the restroom with them, or even share water fountains. We did share the bus, but blacks went to the back of the bus. And yes, we used the N-word, not in a mean, hateful way, but that's the word we were taught by our parents.

Was it wrong for white people to deny black people the opportunities and freedom we had? Of course it was, and only a diehard racist would argue otherwise. But progress toward racial equality was made during the 1950s. The 1960s are remembered as the Civil Rights decade because of landmark legislation, including the Civil Rights Act of 1964, Voting Rights Act of 1965, and the Civil Rights Act of 1968, but the impetus for these acts were set in motion in the 1950s through demonstrations, sermons, and speeches that appealed both to reason and to emotion. In 1955 in Montgomery, Alabama, Rosa Parks refused to give up her seat on a bus to a white person. The late-1950s saw the first sit-ins at segregated lunch counters. And in Atlanta, Martin Luther King Jr. began serving as the first president of the Southern Christian Leadership Conference in 1957.

Some of the Southern states and cities vigorously resisted integration, while in others the process was relatively peaceful. In Atlanta, the editors of the Atlanta Constitution and the Atlanta Journal, our daily newspapers, were very liberal. Partly due to their editorials and partly due to Atlanta Mayor William B. Hartsfield's efforts, desegregation was not as turbulent or as violent as it was in other Southern states. By 1963, Atlanta public schools, buses, lunch counters, movie theaters, golf courses, and other public places had been desegregated, for the most part without violence. Atlanta advertised itself as "the city too busy to hate."

Jim Crow laws were state and local laws enacted between Reconstruction and 1965 that mandated segregation of races. State-sponsored school segregation was declared unconstitutional by the Supreme Court of the United States in 1954 in Brown v.

Board of Education, which struck down the "separate but equal" policies of many school systems. The remaining Jim Crow laws were overturned by the Civil Rights Act of 1964 and the Voting Rights Act of 1965.

International relations had a definite effect on the federal government's role in ending discrimination in the US. In the ideological battles for hearts and minds that was a major element of the Cold War, the US had a reputation and an image to maintain around the world. It would have been difficult to portray itself as the leader of the free world when many of its citizens were discriminated against on the basis of race, religion, or ethnicity. This would have been especially damaging in efforts to win over Third World Countries.

In the South, "blockbusting" was a tactic used by real estate agents in the late 1940s through the 1950s to prey on whites' fear of blacks. An agent would buy a house in a white neighborhood and sell or rent the house to a black family. They usually rented them, since many neighborhoods had covenants that prohibited the homeowner from selling to anyone other than whites. These covenants were later struck down by the courts, but during the 1950s, they were in full force. Once people noticed that they had black neighbors, "for sale" signs went up almost overnight in front of every home. Within weeks, an all-white neighborhood became all-black. The 1950s were the years when so called "white flight" began, and this mass movement of whites to the suburbs lasted until well into the 1970s.

In the early morning hours of October 12, 1958, a violent incident shook Atlantans' confidence and caused them to wonder if the city really was too busy to hate. A large bomb exploded next to the Temple, Atlanta's oldest and most prominent synagogue, causing significant damage but no injuries. Although Jews were excluded from some social clubs and organizations, violent acts against Jews were rare in Atlanta. Temple members practiced Reformed Judaism, where they sought to blend in with the community and not stand out as different, which made the bombing even less likely to have been a case of anti-Semitism. As it turned out, the synagogue had a new rabbi, Jacob Rothschild, who was far more liberal than the previous rabbi, and he often made the congregation uncomfortable with his stance against social injustices. Moreover, he was a friend of Martin Luther King Jr., with whom he was often seen, and this almost certainly was the reason for the bombing. Mayor Hartsfield rushed to the Temple and issued a blanket condemnation of both the bombers and the political demagogues who he believed shared the blame. Atlanta Constitution editor Ralph McGill wrote a blistering editorial about the bombing, and President Eisenhower condemned the bombing and offered the support of the FBI in apprehending those responsible. Eventually several men were arrested, and one of them was brought to trial, but he was acquitted, and charges were dropped against the others. It was a miscarriage of justice by an all-white jury, but in hindsight, the outpouring of good will by the people of Atlanta demonstrated that times had changed and that the city was ready to move forward.

After the war, many black workers found jobs in labor-intensive manufacturing industries like automobiles, steel, chemicals, and meatpacking. The majority of these jobs required unskilled labor, but technology advances after World War II eliminated many of these jobs. These jobs had been held by both blacks and whites, but the loss of jobs disproportionately affected blacks. The loss of jobs available to blacks in the Fifties unquestionably contributed to the social unrest and violence of the Sixties.

In movies, entertainment, and broadcast media, blacks were virtually invisible. In movies, blacks had been cast primarily as servants of white people. It took Hollywood a long time to get the message that this was racist and humiliating to blacks. There wasn't a lot of progress until the 1960s, but even then, blacks often played the roles of gangsters and pimps, or at best, as sidekicks to white characters. The 1950s did, however, open the door at least a bit, with black actors and actresses like Sidney Poitier, Harry Belafonte, and Dorothy Dandridge playing starring roles and defying earlier racial stereotyping. In 1954, Dorothy Dandridge was nominated for the Academy Award for Best

Actress for her role in *Carmen Jones* (Grace Kelly won). No black actor or actress won an Oscar in the 1950s, but Sidney Poitier won the Oscar for Best Actor in 1963 for his role in *Lilies of the Field*.

In television, blacks were even less visible than they were in movies. One of the few shows that black entertainers appeared on regularly was *The Ed Sullivan Show*, a mainstay of Sunday night TV from 1948-1971. Network executives and sponsors were initially against appearances by blacks, but the feared backlash from viewers never materialized. The first TV show to be hosted by a black person was *The Nat King Cole Show*, which debuted on NBC in November 1956. Even with the popularity of Cole and the entertainers – both black and white - who appeared with him, the show only lasted one year due to the lack of national sponsorship.

There was one black TV show that was so controversial that it cannot be ignored: *Amos 'n' Andy*. Beginning as a radio show in 1928 and moving to CBS-TV in 1951, the situation comedy ran for two seasons and was shown as reruns until 1966. Set in Harlem, the show centered on the activities of George "Kingfish" Stevens, a conniver who was always looking for ways to make a fast buck. The NAACP protested that the show was offensive in its depiction of blacks, and the show was canceled after the second year. *Amos 'n' Andy* continued to be shown in reruns, but by the mid-1960s, the growing civil rights movement brought increased pressure on CBS, and the network withdrew the show.

Black athletes fared little better in a segregated society than entertainers. There were a few black athletes in major college sports prior to the 1950s, but with many colleges and universities segregated until the 1960s, there was little opportunity for black athletes. Some schools had "gentlemen's agreements" that coaches would not recruit blacks. Southern schools would sometimes refuse to play schools with black athletes on their teams. The first black athletes who played at largely white schools often endured taunting from opponents and segregation both at home and on the road. By the end of the Fifties, however, an ever-increasing number of black athletes were playing at major schools except in the South, where integration did not come until the 1960s. Once black athletes demonstrated their abilities, however, the floodgates opened and by the beginning of the 1970s, most major colleges were actively recruiting black athletes.

Black athletes had marginally better success in breaking the color barrier in professional sports. Jackie Robinson broke the color barrier of major league baseball in 1947 when he started at second base for the Brooklyn Dodgers. By 1958, every major league baseball team had at least one black player. The National Football League (NFL) was integrated in 1946, but not until 1962 would all NFL teams have black players on their rosters. In basketball, several teams in the National Basketball Association (NBA) hired black players in 1950, and by the end of the decade there were many black players, including all-time greats Bill Russell and Wilt Chamberlain.

In national politics, blacks had had little success in Congressional elections in the twentieth century. In 1950, there were no blacks in the US Senate, and only two blacks in the US House. The first black US Senator in modern times was not elected until 1966, and only four blacks have been elected in all (three of them from Illinois). Blacks have considerably more representation in the House, with more than ninety elected since 1950, the majority of these from black-majority districts, and all but two being Democrats. With the election of Barack Obama as President in 2008, a huge barrier was broken.

The 1950s did not end with equality for blacks, but the way had been paved for the struggles of the 1960s that resulted in equal opportunity for all, at least under the law. In some parts of the country, these struggles were violent and bloody, while in other areas, desegregation and an end to discrimination were accomplished largely through nonviolence and in a relatively peaceful manner.

CHAPTER 12

War (Hot and Cold)

With 70 million people killed during World War II and with the atomic bomb such a threat, many people thought that it was the end of war, that people would not be insane enough to go through that scale of carnage and destruction again. But even before Germany surrendered in May 1945, it was apparent that the Soviet Union would be our ideological and military enemy in the post-war period. In 1949, when the Communist forces under Mao Zedong (we called him Mao Tse-tung then) defeated the Nationalist forces of Chiang Kai-shek, we added China to our list of enemies in what was dubbed the "Cold War" in a 1947 speech by former FDR advisor Bernard Baruch.

One phrase that was heard a lot during the 1950s was "displaced person." The term referred to the millions of people who were forcibly taken from their own countries as prisoners or slave labor during World War II. The majority of these were from Eastern Europe. Throughout the 1950s, refugee agencies worked to return these people to their native countries and to their families if any other family members survived the war and its aftermath. The Immigration and Nationality Act of 1952 removed some of the barriers to foreign-born people becoming US citizens, and many DPs, as they were called, immigrated to the United States, which gave them sanctuary.

Another major post-war development was the establishment of the State of Israel. Zionists had been pouring into Israel, or Palestine as it was called then, for decades, despite the British attempts to keep them out. After the war ended, the United Nations recognized the new State of Israel in 1948.

The uneasy peace at the end of World War II lasted less than five years. On June 25, 1950, North Korean military forces crossed the 38th parallel into South Korea, and soon afterward, the US was back in a shooting war. With the Chinese supporting the North Koreans, and the Soviets supporting China, it was a long, bloody war that finally ended three years later in 1953. Never again did American forces directly face Soviet or Chinese troops, but over the next few decades there would be numerous proxy wars where the US supported groups fighting against Communists, and the Communists supported groups fighting against the US or our allies. As a kid, I was blissfully unaware of the war that was raging on the other side of the world, but my mother had me trying to improve my reading by tackling the newspaper while I was in the first grade. One of the first words I learned from the newspaper was "Korea," since it was in the headlines a lot.

The biggest proxy war happened two thousand miles from South Korea, where the French were fighting to maintain control of French Indochina, a longtime French colony. With the French surrender at Dien Bien Phu in 1954 and the subsequent treaty that divided Indochina into North and South Vietnam, the war was over. President Eisenhower, in a news conference, stated his belief in the so called "Domino Theory," speculating that if one country in a region fell to communism, then the surrounding countries would follow in a domino effect. This became US policy for subsequent administrations to justify American intervention around the world. At the time, however, few Americans had any inkling that the United States would be at war in Indochina within a few years.

In the aftermath of the war, with the Soviet Union taking over the countries in Eastern Europe, Americans feared that the Communists were bent on world domination. However, even with clear evidence that the Soviet Union was a brutal, totalitarian regime, some Americans were sympathetic to Communism. Many of these Americans were actors and writers, and some of them had actually joined the Communist Party before the war. In the US Congress, the House Un-American Activities Committee (HUAC) investigated alleged Communist sympathizers, including actors and writers, politicians, union officials, and even military leaders. Senator Joseph McCarthy worked with HUAC to uncover Americans who were believed to be Communists or Communist sympathizers. HUAC "blacklisted" many members of the entertainment industry who refused to cooperate with the committee. When many of McCarthy's accusations against government officials and military leaders could not be proved, he lost favor, and in December 1954, the Senate voted to censure him, ending the period of McCarthyism.

The Atomic Age officially began on July 16, 1945 with the detonation of the first nuclear weapon at Alamogordo, New Mexico. In August 1945, two atomic bombs were used against Japan, the only time that nuclear weapons have been used in war. On August 29, 1949, the Soviet Union successfully tested its first nuclear weapon. The nuclear arms race was on. In 1952 the US detonated the first hydrogen bomb. The following year, the Soviets tested their own hydrogen weapon. Throughout the 1950s, the two countries would blithely test more than two hundred nuclear weapons, most of them in the atmosphere. Unthinkable as it sounds now, most of the US tests were in the deserts of Nevada. Eventually, it was recognized that radioactive fallout was very harmful and that radiation levels in plants and animals were increasing. There was some indication that harmful radioactive isotopes produced in nuclear explosions were present in dangerous amounts in milk. In 1963, the Partial Test Ban Treaty between the US, UK, and the Soviet Union prohibited nuclear testing in the atmosphere, forcing subsequent tests to be underground.

After World War II, there was actually a lot of optimism that nuclear energy could be tamed and put to use benefiting mankind instead of destroying it. It was commonly believed than nuclear electrical power would be so cheap that homes would not even have meters. That never happened of course, and today, more than sixty years later, the US still relies largely on fossil fuels for electrical power production. It was also proposed that nuclear explosives could be used for public works projects. In the US, Operation Plowshare conducted a number of experimental underground nuclear explosions to test concepts, but it was determined that too much dangerous radiation was released and that the cost was too high to justify. At one time, it had been thought that nuclear explosives could be used to widen the Panama Canal or to construct a new sea-level canal.

Now, how did the Atomic Age affect kids? The first effect was the "duck and cover" drill that kids learned at school. Kids were taught that if they saw a bright flash of light, they were to immediately get on the ground under some kind of cover — like their desk — and assume a fetal position, covering their head with their hands. This supposedly would protect you against the shock wave of a nuclear blast, but it gave no protection against heat, radiation, or fallout. In any case, since the USSR did not have operational ICBMs until 1959, we assumed that our radars would pick up enemy bombers far enough out to give us at least two to three hours' warning. Our county had evacuation plans for students, and once during each school year, we had a drill where certain parents, usually mothers who were at home and had a car, came to the school and picked up the kids and drove them to our assigned safe location. For our school, it was the little town of Covington, Georgia, where supposedly there were enough civil defense supplies (food, water, and medicine) to sustain us for a while. In the event that we didn't survive a nuclear attack, we all had to have metal dog tags with our name, address, and date of birth. Mine also has a "P," signifying that if there was enough of me left to bury, it should be a Protestant burial. I still have my dog tags, a memento of the early Atomic Age.

During the early Cold War era, there was a lot of interest in fallout shelters to protect people from bomb blasts and radioactive fallout after a nuclear attack. The US government even encouraged building personal fallout shelters with pamphlets like *You Can Survive*. Many homeowners built shelters or had them built by contractors. Many of these were very basic, but some people spent thousands of dollars on very elaborate shelters, often underground, that were shielded against radiation and contained food, water, and electrical generators. Some of these were designed to keep the occupants safe for a year or more. During the height of fallout shelter construction in the late-1950s and early-1960s, there were serious public debates, some televised, about the morality of keeping your neighbors out even if you had to use firearms to do so. Eventually, people realized that even if a shelter would keep them alive for a few days after an attack, they would eventually have to leave the shelter and be exposed to fatal radiation, so interest in fallout shelters waned. There must be thousands of shelters still in people's backyards.

Post-apocalyptic novels and movies were springing up almost before the fallout settled from Hiroshima. Many of these were science fiction, where radiation has caused mutations in some animals, so we had giant man-eating insects or lizards or swamp creatures. More serious were the stories that described life on earth for humans after a nuclear war. The most influential of these was the 1957 novel *On the Beach* by Nevil Shute. The book, which was made into a movie in 1959, somberly depicted the last survivors from World War III hanging on in Australia while dying from radiation poisoning. The book was considered so important that many daily newspapers in the US serialized it.

Some of the "Red Scare" issues of the 1950s seem silly now. One of these was fluoridation of drinking water to prevent tooth decay. Many people, including right-wing groups such as the John Birch Society, believed that fluoridation was a Communist plot to poison Americans. Longtime Atlanta Mayor William B. Hartsfield was adamant about this, and he refused to allow Atlanta's drinking water to be fluoridated. Only after he left office was the city's water supply fluoridated.

After the Korean War ended in 1953, the United States enjoyed a ten-year period of relative peace, but by the end of the decade, events were in motion that would change that. After leading the Cuban Revolution against dictator Fulgencio Batista, Fidel Castro came to power in 1959 and installed a Communist government with close ties to the Soviet Union. In April 1961, an unsuccessful attempt by US-trained Cuban exiles to invade Cuba and overthrow Castro failed. In October of 1962, US spy planes detected that the Soviet Union was installing intermediate-range ballistic missiles in Cuba. This led to a major showdown as

President John F. Kennedy demanded that the Soviet Union remove the missiles. Kennedy also ordered the US Navy to blockade Cuba and prevent Soviet ships from bringing more missiles into Cuba. For two weeks both nations were toe-to-toe on the brink of war, until finally the Soviets agreed to remove the missiles in exchange for concessions from the US. This was the closest the Cold war came to becoming a nuclear war. I remember the two-week period now called the Cuban Missile Crisis very well. I was sixteen years old, and I can assure you it was scary. During this time, our local radio station kept telling people what to do if we were attacked. One time the announcer slipped up and said "when" instead of "if." In Atlanta, we would have had only a few minutes warning if the Cuban missiles had been launched.

Although the Vietnam War would dominate the 1960s and 1970s, the seeds had been sown in the 1950s. Soon after the French were defeated and left Vietnam, Communist guerillas began trying to overthrow the South Vietnamese government. President Eisenhower pledged his support, but no US combat troops were sent, only a few advisors. President Kennedy, who succeeded Eisenhower, choose to "draw the line in the sand," with South Vietnam to be defended to prevent any more dominoes from falling in Southeast Asia. Little did we know what the consequences would be of that decision.

The Cold War during the Fifties was largely a battle of wills between President Eisenhower and Soviet Premier Nikita Khrushchev, who both took office in 1953. In 1956, while addressing Western ambassadors at a reception at the Polish embassy in Moscow, Khrushchev uttered his famous statement "Whether you like it or not, history is on our side. We will bury you," meaning that communism would triumph over capitalism. Another famous incident involving ideology was the so called "Kitchen Debate" between Khrushchev and Vice President Richard Nixon at the opening of an American exhibition in Moscow in 1959. An entire American-style house was built and filled with the latest recreational and labor saving devices intended to show what life was like for American families. The impromptu debate took place in the kitchen as both men debated the merits of their economic systems. It was generally acknowledged that Nixon won the debate, but both agreed that technological competition was better than military conflict.

During the 1950s, we lived every day with the threat of nuclear annihilation hanging over our heads. But you can't live in a state of constant fear, so after a few years, we got used to the Mutual Assured Destruction (MAD) concept that no one would be crazy enough to launch an attack with nuclear weapons if they knew their side would be destroyed too. At the end of the 1950s decade, only the United States, Great Britain, and the Soviet Union had nuclear weapons. The British were our allies, and although we didn't trust the Soviets, we figured they had enough sense to not start a nuclear war that no one could win. There were times in the following decade that that belief wavered, but at least in the 1950s, MAD gave us some sense of security, ironic as that sounds.

END NOTES

Most people probably think their own coming of age decade was special, and they would be right, but I think there was something truly unique and exceptional about growing up in the 1950s. The decade was almost idyllic compared to the turmoil and social upheavals of the 1960s, which will be remembered for Vietnam, students rioting in the streets, racial unrest, feminists, hippies, free love, communes, heavy metal, the rise of the left wing, and just plain chaos at times. It's true we were the first generation of kids who lived under the daily threat of nuclear annihilation, but we managed to accept it and live with it. It was an era of self reliance and it was the last time a US President could speak the words "Ask not what your country can do for you, ask what you can do for your country," as John F. Kennedy did at his inauguration in January 1961, without being ridiculed.

The 1950s was a decade of exciting changes, some good, some bad. The American standard of living rose steadily during the decade, and Americans had more leisure time than ever. Cars gave Americans the mobility they've always cherished. Television kept millions of people glued to their TV sets, so much so that motion pictures became almost obsolete. When Americans weren't at home watching TV, they had their newfangled transistor radios to take anywhere within range of a radio station. Mothers stayed at home raising their kids and spending hours a day cooking, sewing, and washing, drying, and ironing clothes.

The 1950s was the decade when legally mandated segregation and Jim Crow laws began to crumble. The civil rights movement was underway in earnest, and both blacks and whites marched in the streets and battled in the courts to reverse centuries of bigotry and discrimination. The legal battles were eventually won in the following decade, although discrimination itself exists to some degree even today.

Sometimes I wish that I could slip back in time and savor the slower pace and relative innocence of the Fifties that we lost in the following decades and share it with today's kids. In some ways, life was better then, but in other ways it was harder. But until someone invents a time travel machine, I'll stay in the present and keep on reminiscing about the Fabulous Fifties.

If you really want to take a trip back in time to see for yourself what the Fifties were like, check out *A Christmas Story*, a 1983 film classic that's spot-on in depicting what life was like for a boy growing up in the United States during the Fifties. Ralphie Parker, the main character, is all of us.

And if I learned anything that's worth passing on, it's to never throw anything away. The toys, games, magazines, comic books, and baseball cards that I had as a kid would be worth a fortune today on eBay!

* * * * * *

In 1978, at the age of thirty-two, I decided it would be a cool thing to jump out of an airplane, so I went to a parachute center south of Atlanta, went through a day of training, and made my first jump. I liked it so much that I went back a couple of times a month for the next two years to do it some more. Eventually I bought my own parachute, a very old and well used Mark I Paracommander. The Paracommander was one of the best round canopies ever made, but it had to be packed just right, or it would malfunction. In October 1980, I was making a jump, and after free-falling from 5,000 feet, I pulled the ripcord at 2,000 feet. The canopy started to open, then I went into a very high-speed spin because one of the canopy suspension lines had looped over the canopy, preventing it from opening properly. The Paracommander, which was very similar to the parachutes used for parasailing at beaches, has dozens of propulsion openings in it, and with the openings on one side of the canopy closed, the other openings were causing the parachute to spin very fast. Spinning that fast made my hands and arms weigh so much because of centrifugal force that it was very difficult to get one hand in to pull the ripcord of the reserve chute. I was falling very fast. When I finally pulled the ripcord, the reserve canopy flew into the malfunctioning main canopy. All I could think to do was to pull the reserve canopy back down and fling it out. This time the reserve canopy caught air and inflated, and I hit the ground about two seconds later. So it was a very short and exciting trip from a mile high to the ground, and I'll never forget it. It was the stuff of nightmares for the next couple of years, but they gradually faded away. Did I jump again after such an experience? Yes, you have to get back on the horse after falling, and I had to get back on the plane and jump again, which I did thirteen more times before hanging up the ripcord. So that was my most exciting moment that I mentioned in the Foreword.

ABOUT THE AUTHOR

Hello, I'm Jim Chambers, and I wrote this book. If you're interested, here is a brief description of my life.

I was born in Piedmont Hospital in Atlanta, Georgia, on July 22, 1946, exactly nine months and five days after my father returned home from England, where he had served with the U.S. 8th Air Force during World War II. After a relatively undistinguished twelve years in public schools, I went on to the Georgia Institute of Technology, where I earned bachelor's and master's degrees in civil engineering. After that, I went to work with the Georgia Department of Transportation, where I designed highways for thirty-four years. My claim to fame there was being the co-designer of Spaghetti Junction, a huge freeway interchange where I-85 and I-285 cross a few miles northeast of Atlanta. I retired in 2001, and since then, I have continued working part-time for a consulting engineering firm.

I'm an avid reader, reading a little of everything, but I prefer action novels, history and historical fiction, and biography. My wife Deborah and I love to travel, but scuba diving and underwater photography are our real passions. Deborah shoots video, and I shoot stills. I've managed to win or place in several major international underwater photography competitions, and my underwater photography has been published in magazines such as National Geographic and Popular Photography.

I'm slowing down a bit as old age creeps up, not to mention the four major spine surgeries I've had since 2004, but I'm hanging in there. I had so much fun writing this book – my first – that I think I'll write another one.

LaVergne, TN USA
15 October 2009
160977LV00005B/33/P